Advance praise for *Dionysos Speed*

Dionysos Speed is a shot in the eye, a kaleidoscopic hallucinatory satirical rant describing a delirious feverdream of digital disruption and collapse. In short blasts skittering between breathless monologues and mantras, the book is a new apocalypse, in which *Revelations* meets *Nova Express*. It's a jeremiad for the age of AI fantasies & digital conspiracy that just might inoculate its reader against the viral lure of virtual post-humanism. Read it before you are consumed by the blue light!

Stuart Kendall

If the target of *Dionysos Speed* is the "integrative, unitary capitalism" which absorbs, assimilates, & regurgitates everything in its production of consensual reality, the book's devices are phantasmagoric images, striking associations: now raw visions, now elaborate manifestos punctuated with outbursts of (nonsense) poetry, drawing on the full range of avant-garde gestures & operations, and reminding of their creative disruptive rage in their attempt to smash in the façade of naturalized representations that bar us from confronting and undergoing the experience of the real — of what remains in excess of our cognitive rigging, of what refuses to be reified into screenable info content, troubling and unassimilable, flipping over the known into unknown. Again & again, the book urges us to follow its envisioned terrorists, anarchist artists, or punk rockers: "cultivate your legitimate strangeness."

Erika Mihálycsa

DIONYSOS
SPEED

DIONYSOS
SPEED

Rainer J. Hanshe

Contra Mundum Press   New York · London · Melbourne

Dionysos Speed
© 2024 Rainer J. Hanshe

First Contra Mundum Press
Edition 2024.

Library of Congress
Cataloguing-in-Publication
Data

Hanshe, Rainer J.
Dionysos Speed / Rainer J.
Hanshe

—1st Contra Mundum Press
Edition

192 pp., 6 × 9 in.

ISBN 9781940625676

   I. Hanshe, Rainer J.
  II. Title.

2023948215

CONTENTS

Our prehistoric life began amidst enforested gloom with the abandonment of the protected instinctive life of nature. We sought, instead, an adventurous existence amidst the crater lands and ice fields of self-generated ideas. Clambering onward, we have slowly made our way out of a maze of isolated peaks into the level plains of science. Here, one step seems definitely to succeed another, the universe appears to take on an imposed order, and the illusions through which mankind has painfully made its way for many centuries have given place to the enormous vistas of past & future time. The encrusted eye in the stone speaks to us of undeviating sunlight; the calculated elliptic of Halley's comet no longer forecasts world disaster. The planet plunges us through a chill void of star years, and there is little or nothing that remains unmeasured.

— **Loren Eiseley,** *The Unexpected Universe*

The sailors' hydrarchy was defeated in the 1720s, the hydra beheaded. But it would not die. The volatile, serpentine tradition of maritime radicalism would appear again and again in the decades to come, slithering quietly below decks, across the docks, and onto the shore, biding its time, then rearing its head unexpectedly in mutinies, strikes, riots, urban insurrections, slave revolts, and revolutions.

— **Marcus Rediker** *&* **Peter Linebaugh,** *The Many-Headed Hydra: The Hidden History of the Revolutionary Atlantic*

There is nothing I abominate and shit upon so much as this idea of representation, that is, of virtuality, of non-reality, attached to all that is produced & shown ... as if it were intended in this way to socialize and at the same time paralyze monsters, make the possibilities of explosive deflagration which are too dangerous for life pass instead through the channel of the stage, the screen, or the microphone, and so turn them away from life.

— **Antonin Artaud,** *To have done with the judgment of god*

DIONYSOS SPEED

THE TERROR OF
NARCISSUS

THE TERRIFYING, CATACLYSMIC SOUND of over 8 billion mirrors cracking, splintering, shattering into pieces reverberates throughout every locale on earth, a piercing, eerie sound whose decibels test the tympana. The central nervous system of most is scored; the psyche disordered; the eyes emaciated. The animal kingdom is thrust into states of delirium at the alarming noise: birds and other animals shrieking, howling, grunting, each animal uttering its primal intonation.

When gazing into the array of shimmering fragments of silvered glass: — images of the self split into endless discordant pieces gaze back, the degrees of curvature & vergence broken, the schismatic wavelengths of light now disorienting, distorting more than carnival mirrors — sharpness, lines, colors, contrasts no longer intact but, shivered, twisting in, twisting out, of: clearness, wholeness, distinction. The optics of vision become kaleidoscopic, hallucinatory, vertiginous.

From the fragments stripped of silvering, the gaze plummets into nothingness, into glass, where all temporality is lost. What gazes back? *Nothing but nothingness.*

Bewildered by the loss of mirrors, malnourished and hungry for returning images, the image hungry seek out reflecting objects of every kind, from toasters to pots to puddles to glassy ash trays to other dark yet shiny surfaces, but none of these surrogate echoes satisfy the urge, let alone satiate the desire for the clear doubling of the self that had been cut into the flesh since the birth of the camera & intensified to the *nth* degree, cubed to the power of mania, with the pervasive interlacing of social media into the fabric of every aspect of existence, into flesh, organs, cellular system, neural network.

Taking out their phones in order to gaze at themselves, the image hungry shoot self-portrait after self-portrait, thumbing their shutters with abandon, repeatedly pressing into their phones with force, as if the intensity of the gesture would guarantee the expected result, only to discover, to their panic, that each returning image was devoid of a head.

Malfunction??

Power off; power on:::::::::reload—update.....

Depressing the buttons on their phones as if paparazzi capturing infinite streams of images, the iris of each camera snaps open-closed with the anxious velocity of a dragonfly :|:|:|:|:|:|:|:|:|:|:|:|:| a barrage of images sputtering forth, shitting into the camera like a contracting and expanding rectum, reducing light to matrixes, pixels, voxels, bit depth, not light burned onto celluloid: an image, but not an image, all of which, too, emerge headless.

System breakdown?? Digital bedlam??

The bewilderment intensifies; the panic deepens.

Scrolling through their phones, they check numerous other databases: in these too, every portrait of themselves is, strangely, *headless.*

A sense of dread such as they have never before experienced seizes them, as if having been eviscerated, or somehow erased, bereft of sustaining oxygen and weakened, like deracinated trees, or clouds broken from the sky, cast to the ground like satellite moons devoid of gravity.

At midnight that night, the amplified sound of a handful of dice rattling together inside a fist is heard rumbling thru-out the world, coursing thru airwaves, interrupting broadcasts, disrupting television shows, disturbing podcasts, unsettling radio & streaming transmissions—an unexpected percussive blast or noise-cluster, the multiple die clacking together vigorously, violently, as if some prodigious atomic force, until, the wrist swiftly snapping back, then forward, cutting space like a conductor's baton, the fingers of the fist unfurling, the die released, soaring into the air, tearing spider webs to pieces, ace, cinque, deuce, cater, sice, trey blurring in time, numbers whorling together, numbers breaking apart

The silence reverberates with palpable intensity through every technological medium as the dice tumble thru the sky, surging thru space-time like a broken constellation — stars dispersed, cut from gravity, whirling chaotically about, numbers in errant motion: cater, cinque, sice, trey, ace, deuce–cinque, ace, sice, trey, deuce, cater–trey, sice, cinque, cater, deuze, ace

until, one by one, like acrobats free of any directional point, the multiple die tumble onto a table: the sound of the tools of play echo outward like the reverberations of a sharply struck snare drum, die after die after die — rapid, random, free of predictability:

some landing

w/one strike,

others tumbling over twice

3 ×

or more

boom

boom

boom-*boom-boom*

boom

boom

boom-boom

boom-*boom*-boom-*boom*-boom

As the last die hits the surface, its thunderous punctuating blow is accompanied by the sound of the sea and crashing waves, of the sputtering, popping, sizzling noises of fire, gases expanding, cellulose breaking down, steam bursting open from wood, the splitting of tectonic plates noising like onslaughts of banging & cracking lightning

With the fall of the die, a new constellation forms, a number born of chaos, which breaks the existing systems of the world into generators of true deviant randomness, shattering the patterned and structured focus of algorithms into pure chaos, all technological mediums gone berserk.

The image of the *subject* in every self-projection database decomposes, is supplanted by the jagged shards, disparate elements, & ludic, disjointed features of terrifying carnivalesque masks, an amalgamation of materials and elements devoid of unifying characteristics, the face made monstrous.

Overcome by this disruption & rending of their images, the self-addicts possessed by the mania for infinite replication are set into frenzies. Seized by the irresistible force of the masks, they begin engaging in disjunctive movements and vehement gestures bordering on madness, tragico-absurd dances wherein revolt is given energetic physical expression. The anamorphic figuration of the face takes action in the fractured body—all control is lost, infection takes over, mania erupts, giving birth to streams of disordered ecstasy.

THE LAUGHING
VULTURE

THE first missive that went out that day read:

F m s b w t ö z ä u pggiv — ..? mü

Believing it to be nothing more than nonsense, a technical mishap, the keyboard gone accidentally amok, almost everyone deleted it, but when sending out a new message of their own, the moment it was deployed, what they wrote was immediately transformed into this second missive:

In the beginning was the Word, and the Word was with ...

Although slightly bewildered by the event, this apparently spiritual alteration of their message was considered nothing more than an irritant, the invasive gesture of a pesky religious hacker. Merely aggravated, each person deleted this transmission & sent out another message of their own, only to find that it, too, was immediately transformed into this third missive:

zdouc nfoùnfa mbaah

Was this yet more gibberish, another technical snafu, or some bastardization of an African, Indian, or other tongue, a coded message preceding a phishing attack?

When entering the phrases into a translation engine, the machine thought it was Kannada, but it wasn't, and the text resisted translation, with not even a single syllable differing from the original.

Their mouths growing dry, their pupils dilating, exasperation intensifying, each person sent out yet another message, but what emerged resembled nothing that any of them had typed:

... from some alien energy the visions come:

What in the hell is this? many wondered, some UFO freak pranking them? A gang of physicist hackers engaging in digital flash mob acts?

Quickly sending out another message, what appeared in its stead was but more gibberish:

gadjama tuffm i zimzalla binban

Disoriented and nauseous, questioning whether what they were typing was not what they were typing, or if they were hallucinating, or delirious, or if their eyesight was going, each person deleted the strange missive and sent out another message of their own, carefully examining each letter as they frantically thumbed it in, then pressed send, only to be met with a missive they found exceedingly disturbing:

Sooner murder an infant in its cradle than nurse unacted desires.

Terrified by this statement, fearing they would be considered immoral, or deranged, they quickly deleted the missive and ran a virus scan, but no malware was detected.

Picking at their skin, swiftly losing the ability to control their impulses, discernment faltering, nose running, the inability to generate messages of their own was giving birth to violent sensations.

As if trying to control chaos through sheer velocity, as if speed alone might undermine interference, each person generated a slew of further messages, but every single one of them was mutated into another unwanted missive. It began with this instance of gibberish:

gramma berida bibala glandri galassassa

However, after a parody of Genesis:

In the beginning was the Image, & the Image was with ...

further messages were not transformed into words, but images, a near-violent barrage of them, from pure black to disparate points of white light, to clouds of nebula-like hues, to indescribably phantasmagoric bursts of color, to black & so on, flickering at accelerated speeds, entering the body, altering perception, image become music.

While these lambent images were resonating through every screen, after emerging from their trances and attempting to send out another post, it came back blank, a wordless void almost more terrifying than each of the preceding seizures of their posts.

Frantic, many thought the system itself must be breaking down, & after attempting to make another post, were relieved to see their words appear, but then, almost instantly, they evaporated — in place of them, the following missive arose:

In the beginning was the Sound, & the Sound was with ...

Thereafter, every following message was not supplanted with images, nor with words, but with a series of eerie, unsettling sounds — first, a high-pitched glossolaliac elongation of seemingly indiscernible words, extending for what felt like an interminable period of time, at decibels that made their devices rattle, then, sounded with searing ferocity & uttered with detonating force, the ceaseless repetition of two syllables, jettisoned from the palate like a burst of rapid-fire bullets, enunciated ad infinitum, in a piercing crescendo and decrescendo, followed by nothing but pure frequencies, tones whose vibrations, after having entered the nervous system, rearranged its molecules. Then, another enigmatic missive emerged:

It is upon us: — a new mystery sings in your bones.
Develop your legitimate strangeness.

Immediately, people changed their passwords, rebooted their devices, logged into their accounts again, sent out new messages, but these, too, underwent mutation.

One after another, upon the immediate clicking of the send button, as their muscles began to ache and their heart rates increased, each new message instantly transformed before their eyes, like some act of digital prestidigitation, into yet some other odd, disturbing pronouncement, from babbled jumbles of letters to cryptic utterances, to sounds, images, anti-humanistic proclamations, and so on:

Beyond a certain point there is no return.

gadji beri bin blassa

"I" do not exist. Who am I? A stranger here and always.

Audio: the sound of a bow shock reverberating through space.

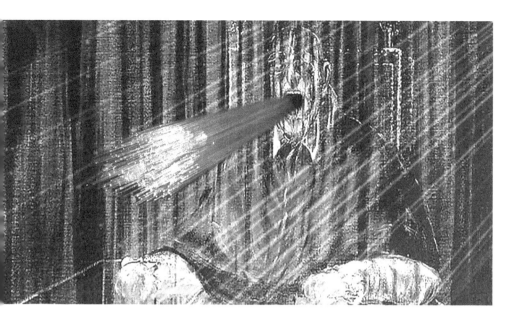

For the brief span of an hour am a different person.

gluglamen gloglada gleroda glandridi

... no more word scripts, no more flesh scripts

Audio: The sound of black holes merging.

The great and crescive self, rooted in absolute nature,
supplants all relative existence and ruins the kingdom
of mortal friendship & love.

wulubu ssubudu uluwu ssubudu

The voices of the world becoming quieter & fewer

Audio: The sound of the noises of the sun.

What did these cryptic interferences imply? Why were they being sent out, and by whom? Beyond *what* point is there no return?? And what does that mean?? Was this event indicative of something apocalyptic, or was it a mere prank?

Growing infuriated and disturbed, fearing that their accounts, or worse, their phones or computers, had been taken over, each person checked the accounts of their friends and followers only to find that, the very same missives appeared on every single account of the system.

Delirious as they were, alternating between oscillating moods and drowsy and wakeful states of consciousness, when an intelligible transmission came through, since it expressed something emotional, a *feeling*, an explanation of behavior, people first believed it was a genuine message that they themselves had written, but that in fact was not the case:

> I know everything hasn't been quite right with me, but I can assure you now, very confidently, that it's going to be all right again. I feel much better now.

In fact, the accounts of statesmen, politicians, presidents, and what people called 'influencers' had each been compromised, and this following missive, as every other, appeared on every single account of the entire system, too:

Mind is gone to the dogs who think incorrigibly in terms of the present. RUB OUT THE WORD

The unnerving, silent act of over 450 million short bursts of inconsequential information being rewritten reverberated thruout every user on earth, an uncanny, almost metaphysical sensation whose effects agitated the nerves, shocking the organs of the body. The central nervous system of many was scored; their psyches disordered; minds irritable, heart rates amplified, mouths parched. The site became a combustion engine of material, a seeming autonomous generator of words, images, sounds, inserting, cutting, interjecting, infiltrating, disrupting all transmissions, cutting the line, short-circuiting communication, the very structure of the site itself off-kilter, its logo morphing from a sweet, innocuous bird into a laughing vulture, text upside down, sideways, angled obliquely, the golden mean gone haywire, making people wonder if these gestures were the result of a cyber attack put into effect by the Russians, the Chinese, or ISIS, but since the content did not seem political in nature (or was it?), perhaps some clan of æsthetico-poetic-anarchist hackers were behind the event, or perhaps it was a prank on the part of the company behind the interface, but that was improbable, and when the confines of the system cracked yet further after a missive of inordinate length was generated thru every single user, far beyond its allotted character count, true panic began to set in:

In the beginning was the Logos, and the Logos was with ... — In the beginning was the Image, and the Image was with ... — In the beginning was the Sound, & the Sound was with ... — And then came the "Logos," yet the Logos was not yet a word but still an Image, and the Eikon was with the shepherds & the farmers and the scribes, and the Eikon was baked like bread in the sun or in furnaces, and life was an arrow, and then the grain record became a thought record and a mythos and a poetics — And then the Eikon became audible, and thought was no longer cuneiform but hieroglyphic & abstract & concrete, and pictograms & phonograms & determinatives gave complexity & shape to ideas & thought was human & birdlike and boustrophedonic and it did not burden the eye, ... *and so on and on*, from stone to copper tablet to papyrus, scroll, volumen, parchment and vellum, to wax-covered slate, codex, book and periodical, from flint, brushes, swabs, hide-cut stencils and the human hand to chisel, stylus, reed brush and goose quill to steel- and gold-nibbed and fountain pens, from the hand to the hand press to the metal press to the linotype, from the typewriter to the ballpoint, from the word to *the word processor*, from Akkadian to Egyptian to Phoenician to Gothic to Humanist to Digitalist — to write from right to left, left to right, boustrophedonically, and vertically, is to think, conceive, and dream in such manner — but in no longer thinking from right to left, or from left to right, let alone boustrophedonically, in scrolling infinitely, neurocognitive degeneration sets in: grey matter in decay, impulse control in decay, self-governing in decay, control in ascent, cortico-striatal dopaminergic systems in mutation, the body seized, rewired, threaded into, colonized, the central nervous system less & less one of nerves and more & more one of optics, *the Central Fiber Optick System*— HYPERLINK: NOTIFICATION: PROMPT: INFORMA- TION REWARD: SWITCH-SWITCH-SWITCH: SKIN CONDUCTANCE AROUSAL PEAK—DIGITAL OR- GASM, NO SWEAT, MAN—TAB UPON TAB UPON TAB UPON TAB—GET THE FIX: DIGITAL-COKE-CRACK- SMACK-FENTANYL——FEED THE ALGEBRA OF NEED, GENERATE THE COGNITIVE DEFICIT, DESTROY PRE-FRONTAL GREY MATTER, BURN OUT THE ATTENTIONAL SCOPE::::KILL DURÉE KILL TIME::::::::KILL CHANCE:::::::::KILL BOOK, KILL WORD, KILL BODY—speech now monosyllabic, chopped, not aphorism, haiku, or apothegm, not maxim or epigram, not adage, koan, or proverb, not even gregueria, but brachycephalic gibberish, the extreme mutilation of language. The logos, punktuashun, gone amok: — not poetic, not an ars poetica, but an arse- pudendum, shitting teratoidic shards of letters that seem to be language but resemble it less and less, till the word becomes picture again, yet not hieroglyph, not cuneiform, not an extension of the hand, not an evolution of calligraphy, but extreme abbreviation, thought stuttered, stunted, broken, devoid of breath, bereft of oxygen, become emoticon, machines of in- fantile affect. Now I know my ABCs, now I don't, now I won't, articulate, express, refine, I willfully deform... next time won't you shit with me.

Dai-sy, dai-sy...

THE STRANGE BODY

SINCE THEY WERE ALWAYS ETERNALLY connected, since they were in a constant state of update, reacting instantaneously to notifications, reminders, pop-ups, toasts, opt-in messages, alerts et alia, their reflexes were cybernated down to micro-levels, their physiology rewired, fiber opticked, as if their digital watches were directly connected to their pulses—whether its amplitude was strong and forceful or weak and thready was inconsequential; what was vital was the man-machine unity, the new hybrid evolution of the species that freed itself from its animal heritage to move toward digital perfection, to the 2.0 futures where even death could be surpassed, for death was nothing less than an outmoded biological construct. The central nervous system was no longer central, no longer rooted in the body alone, but fashioned into a more complex network, extending outward, into the greater spatial domain of fiber optics, which itself extended inward into every corpus, so every single bodily unit was united, connected, hyper-linked, making it a digital system, one vast component in an immense, global network of human and machine where everything is artificial & hyperreal, not surreal, not some murky, obscure, unconscious primordiality, but more real than real, enhanced, like digital photos, which, stripped of light and made pure number, became smoother, sharper, clearer, free of imperfection, accident, chance. *Clean.* And since they always know exactly what time it is, know the hour, second, and sub-seconds of time ticking on their digital clock faces, for, with their watches being synched to satellites, time for them is always exact, precise, quantitative and quantifiable, measurable down to the milli-second, to the atto-, zepto-, or yocto-second, down even to Planck time, which, if they want to, they can calculate with their humano-digital corpuses, hence they knew the very exact moment, as well as their latitude and longitude, when they came upon the strange, bewildering object and pinged the location.

At first, they weren't sure what it was; it seemed like a massive lump of matter coiled in the street, something archaic, something lacking fiber optics, something peculiar and deviant, that is, devoid of digitality, a natural or organic entity subject to death.

Since having deactivated their sense of smell as but one of the many machinic refinements of the body, for most of the senses were not deemed vital evolutionary elements (in being too bound to organic matter, to corporeality, the senses did not accord with digital spiritualism), they did not detect the entity as early as organic humans, or animals, would have, but its scent was potent, an amalgamation of cadaverine and putrescine odors: decayed flesh, feces, rotting cabbage, & a foul, garlic-like odor. Clearly, it was a dead body — enzymes had begun eating the cells from the inside out & fetid gases were being released from its intestines. A rank, vile event of the organic world, something almost entirely anachronistic, rarely encountered, proving all the more the necessity of divesting themselves of organicity. Life was less messy that way. The digito-human had no concern for immortality, a concept too linked to anthropomorphism and the natural world. Mortality was not a consideration, for the fragile balancing point between life and death had been excised, and so the fear of death was meaningless, an affective tremor from which they no longer suffered. To even think of extension in terms of immortality was to still be bound to mortality instead of advancing into digital extensivity, to moving beyond humanoid linguistic biases. The digito-human could always be updated and enhanced, consequently, it no longer suffered from existential crises, which were also considered outmoded emotional affects rooted in biologism. A fatal weakness of the species, an irrational element or unpruned evolution that slipped into its DNA coding like a virus unknowingly injected by a spy, an out-of-protocol event finally caught & discarded. For them, meaning was not a concern, but utility, functionality, processor speed, memory capacity (cache memory, RAM, Dynamic RAM, Static RAM, etc.). The object before them was therefore no different from a museum relic or plant.

Despite its active state of decay, it had not yet reached the stage of skeletonization, and when the nude corpse was examined, sufficient enough flesh remained for them to notice that the body had two vertical scars on its back, on the inside of the scapular blades, closest to its spine, and it was almost entirely bald, save for some hair at the front of the head, making them think it was probably a male human from the punk or new wave subculture, each of whom had resisted the advancement of the species into the hyper-digital epoch. Throwbacks to nature, like the loincloth-clad tribes of the jungle who still cooked over fires in the midst of the computer age — such primitive people did not realize that there was actually no reason to even have to eat, that the digestive system too could be eliminated, which therefore emancipated the body from the acts of micturition and defecation, making the digito-humans into machinic angels of a kind. *Pure.* And far beyond the mundane dilemma of eating, to attain the absolute height of digito-spirituality, they no longer endured the indignity of inter faeces et urinam nascimur, for birth itself was freed from placental muck, and so too women from the biological prejudice of generation & the bias of menstruation.

In further examining the body, they discovered that it was clutching a knife in its right hand, as if it had died defending itself against some act of barbarism.

Was it not swift enough with its weapon to survive the attack? Or was it overcome by too many enemies?

If he had moved beyond the organic body, he would never have suffered the threat of death and the pestiferous scent of his entrails would not have marked the street. Something of the sheer bulk and muscularity of the body was however impressive, as if it had been one of the more olympian members of its species. It couldn't then have been of the punk or new wave tribe, for they lacked such vigorously sculpted physicality, hence it was probably an athlete, for many of them also refused the digitization of their bodies & so remained what the digitos dubbed geanderthals. The determination of its identity was ultimately inconsequential. The remains were gathered & eliminated in a smokeless incinerator.

REVERSAL OF THE SIGNS

If the usurping of a system is typically brief — control is recovered within moments, if not hours, making all such anarchic incursions ultimately inconsequential, *de minimus* ruptures that are absorbed, neutralized with little to no significant detriment or change —, the continued presence of the laughing vulture and the obliquely angled, distorted text of the site persisted, just as did the final broken word of the last missive, which reappeared ad infinitum: *dai-sy, dai-sy, dai-sy…*

In this instance, the seizure or breach of control was more lasting, and all efforts at retrieving control continued to prove fruitless, vexing the owners, though even more the users, whose itch to transmit posts had been hardwired into their nerves through incessant use of the device. Bereft of the medium, reward impulse cut — the sweats, anxiety, muscle aches, nausea, hot flashes, tremors, irritability, *the jones.*

Every now and then, the company logo would return, and for a moment, restoration was in sight — *relief, relief* —, but it was a ruse, and the company's breach of the seizure was swiftly stymied, with the cute blue bird forming back into a vulture as the unhinged, maniacal laughter of a Lachsack resounded across the platform, plunging many users into violent frenzies, resulting in the destruction of their devices and other acts of demolition, their synapses buckling under the torsional pain, turning them bestial.

For days, amidst the remnants of the shattered mirrors, the vestiges of which were omnipresent, sharp unsettling reminders of the addictive power of the echo, of doubling, of the craving for self-representation — *junk is image, image is junk* — led many to painstakingly seek to reconstruct their mirrors.

The destruction was so extreme however that reconstruction was well nigh impossible, or led to severe wounding, with shards of glass entering the flesh, like micro-hosts seeking to take it over, the skin scarred, roughened, ravaged, bleeding, the body become part human, part broken mirror: anthropo-speculum, the glassy, vitrified species in vitriolic revolt against all recalcitrant silver, an element they began to have disgust for when it did not obey their desires.

Smash! Again smash, smash!

Yet, when anything remotely resembling a completed puzzle of a shattered mirror was realized, the new object did not act like a mirror — instead of generating a reflection of the body's surface, as if by an act of magick, or technological mutation, or some disorder of reality itself, as if common chemical elements began to function otherwise, it displayed the shocking corridor of the innards, of pulsing kidneys, burbling stomachs, throbbing pancreases, and other organs and bodily networks, provoking sensations of extreme physical revulsion. Facial lineaments were replaced with radiographs of the skull (eye sockets, jaw bones, nasal cavities, cranial structures), the curvature of the buttocks became but meat-like striations of sinew, turning all self-objectifying objects into anatomy book specimens, or butcher's goods, human charcuterie for the image cannibals, provoking increasing disgust for the self-enclosed feedback loop of the ever-repeating echo of the self whose return ceased to return, thereby potentially opening the self to the world instead of closing it perpetually in upon itself, but in its Mobius circuit of self-addiction, the self-enclosed self desired nothing but itself, making such creatures planarians of a sort, polychætes, turbellarians, sea stars, or rather, *fungi.*

Images — millions of images — That's what I eat — Cyclotron shit — I got orgasms — I got screams — I got all the images any hick poet ever shit out — My Power's coming — My Power's coming — My Power's coming — And I got millions & millions & millions of images of Me, Me, Me, meee.

While the fungi were evanescing in a space devoid of echœs, and continually checking the site to attempt to reassert their identity, the image was evaporating before their thumbs, and so the politicians of identity politics were losing grip, but reality was never in their purview, and the world discovered that it wasn't only the site itself that had been breached, but the building too, and outside and within its headquarters, the physical logo had been altered, incensing the owners, who saw it less as a crime and more as an act of desecration. The gesture was the onset of a series of global acts of graffiti of sorts, yet, unlike tagging, these gestures were far more subversive and radical, not the mere reinscription of ego, not another replication and multiplication of the self, but wide scale global revolts inflected with dadaesque & cubist mutations, whereby corporate logos were defaced, distorted, altered, sometimes riddled with nails, paint cans, torn fabrics, or other objects of rough & extreme textures. In acts of mockery and satire, logos were set askew, inverted, overwritten, as were audio presentations of products, with commercials, slogans, and corporate proclamations undergoing possession, short-circuited by burps, farts, shrieks, howls, and discordant noises, as well as all manner of forbidden expressions and unspeakable violations of social norms, mattress commercials intercut with extreme erotic scenes, etchings of Sadean acts in slow motion, church sermons intercepted with digressions on physics, chemistry, cosmology, geology, biology, paleontology, genetics, archæology, and history, political speeches on the necessity of war intersected with violent aural tapestries of sound, from discharging guns to whirrs of aerial vehicles, air raid sirens, thumps of shellfire, roars of rockets, buzzing drones, thuds of artillery shells, improvised explosive devices going off, machineguns rattling, the supersonic crack of bullets, windows smashing, rockets whooshing, grenades exploding, fire hissing, mortar shells detonating, blast waves booming, the clamor of high decibel crunching, sputtering flames, and white noise, the ceaseless crackle of radios, the whirl of generators, and silence, long, extended periods of the most dreadful silence, sheer terror interspersed by boredom, *dead air*, the most unsettling sonic event of all ~

The incursions extended into other domains as well, with the continuous interruption of streaming services on every platform, whose programming was mutated into a roulette wheel of true chaos and randomness, all algorithmic patterns broken, disrupted, intersected, cut—

coupled with a loop of a Lachsack laugh was the first image to short-circuit each network, & thereafter, at unexpected intervals programs were bisected, interspersed, spliced, entirely broken by, washed over, flooded with, subliminally infected, chaotically disrupted, & dissolved into

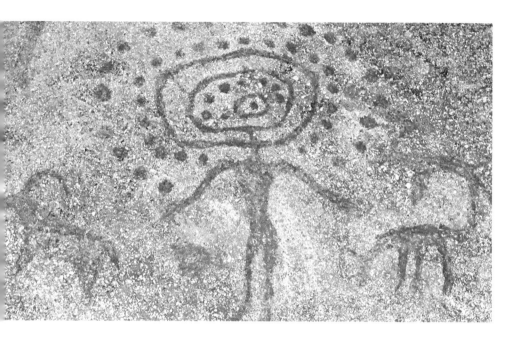

Turning and turning in the widening gyre
Things fall apart; the centre cannot hold;
Mere anarchy is loosed upon the world,
& everywhere
& everywhere
& everywhere

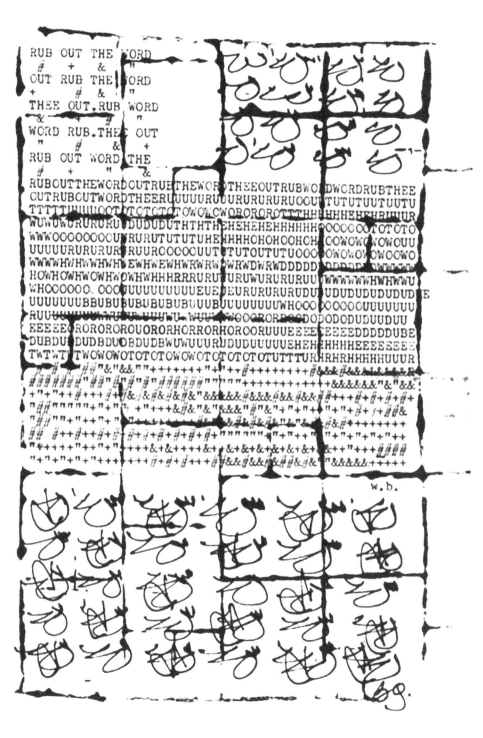

```
RUB OUT THE WORD
 #    +   &   "
OUT RUB THE WORD
 +   #   &   "
THEE OUT.RUB WORD
 &   +   #    "
WORD RUB.THEE OUT
 "        &    +
RUB OUT WORD THE
 #          &

RUBOUTTHEWORDOUTRUBTHEWORDTHEEOUTRUBWORDWORDRUBTHEE
OUTRUBOUTWORDTHEERUUUUURUUURURURURUOOUTUTUTUUTUUTU
TTTTTUUUUUOOTOTOTOTOTOWOWCWOROROROTTTHHHHHEHEHRUUUR
WUWUWURURURUUDUDUDUTHTHTHEHEHEHEHHHHHOOOOOOOTOTOTO
WWWOOOOOOOOUURURURUTUTUTUHEHHHHOHOHOOHOHCOWOWOWOWOUU
UUUUUURURURURRUUROOOCOUUTTUTOUTUTUOOOCOWOWOWOWCOOWO
WWWWHWHWWHHEWHWEWHWRWRWOWRWDWRWDDDDDDDDDDDWWUUU
HOWHOWHWOWHWOWHWHHHRRURUTURUWURURURUUWWWWWWHWHWWU
WHOOOOOOOOOOUUUUUUUUUUUUEUEUEURURURURUDUUDUDUDUDUDUDDUE
UUUUUUUBBUBUBUBUBUBUBUUUBUUUUUUUUUWHOOOOOOOOOOUUUUUUU
RUUUUUUUUUWUUUURUUUWUWUUUWOOOROROOODODODODUDUUDUU
EEEEEOROROROROUOROROHORRORHOROORUUUEEEEEEEEEDDDDDUBE
DUBDUUDUDBDUOBDUDBWUWUUURUDUDUUUUUEHEHEHHHHEEEEEEEE
TWTWTTWOWOWOTOTOTOWOWOTOTOTOTOTUTTTURHRHRHHHHHUUUR
```

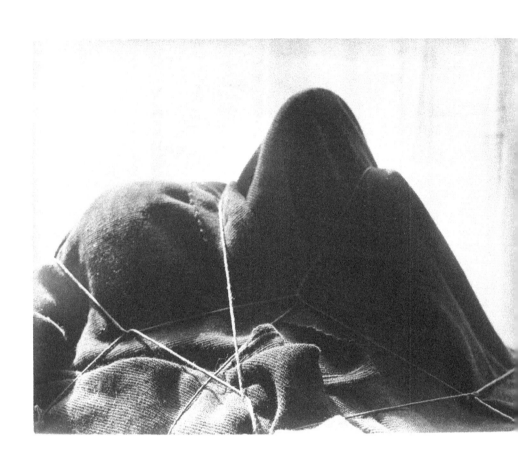

a battery of images, sounds, *&* fragments of music flit through screens around the world, from Hoch's *Cut with the Kitchen Knife*, Avraamov's the *Symphony of Factory Sirens*, and Grosz's *The Agitator* to *Un chien andalou*, recitations of Lesbos and Femmes damnés, loops of *Black Ice*, and *Quattro diversi modi di morire in versi*, to those dreaded days, sometimes weeks, like in war, when the crackle of radios *&* the whirl of generators is cut dead, like a strip of film being cut, *&* instantaneously, everything stops: image, sound, reality: *all the mechanisms are short-circuited*—

MEMORY SURGERY

Still plagued by the Œdipus Complex? That Electra thing got you down? *Don't hang on to biologism!* Get free of the family chains!

DON'T BE A SLAVE TO YOUR PAST!

Can't get Jocasta off your back? Laius just won't let you go? Get free of the mother; get free of the father! End the biologico-humanist dilemma; end the family psychosis! *Join the humano-digitist future!*

DON'T LET BAD MEMORIES RUIN YOUR LIFE!

Frustrated by ambiguous faculties that you don't know how to access or operate? Frustrated by the fleeting power of dreams? Frustrated by the intangibility & limits of fantasizing? Don't suffer from the romanticism of the biologically prejudiced! Forget Kant! Forget antiquated technologies of the self! Learn to access and activate your fiber optick system! Let us help you get mastery & control of your life!

CREATE THE SELF THAT *YOU* DESIRE WITH

DIGITAL MEMORY SURGERY!!

Don't suffer from the dilemmas of bad DNA. Don't suffer from the memory of a bad childhood. With digito-neural surgery, you too can be as free, clean, & as efficient as a computer.

TAKE CONTROL OF YOUR MEMORIES NOW!!

Old lover got you down? Troubled by difficult friends? Can't break free of pesky memories? Don't suffer the endless probings of psychotherapy, psychology, & psychiatry. Don't suffer years and years of trying to break free of complex human dilemmas. The solution is at hand! The solution is electronic! Not medical!

AND IT'S PAIN FREE!

Don't be bound to the archaic vestiges of the psyche. Just as we can search, scan, and clean our computers of malware, we can search, scan, and clean the brain too! Bad memories are just like malware, but we can find threats, quarantine psychological items, & delete them! With digito-neural surgery, not only can bad memories be removed like tumors, but new and improved ones can be implanted.

As part of our evolutionary development, most scientists have realized that psychological complexes are nothing more than vestigial elements no different than appendixes, male nipples, or tails. While some men still have nipples, thankfully, none of us have tails. Why keep bad memories? Extract them like tonsils! Replace them with positive memory implants!

REWIRE YOUR BRAIN FOR OPTIMUM FUNCTIONING! REWIRE YOUR BRAIN *FOR OPTIMISM!* FOR THE BEST OF ALL POSSIBLE SELVES! BECOME PART OF THE OPTIMACY!

In outmoding biologism and shaping our evolutionary future, the brain can be replaced with the perceptron, bad memories can be deleted, disturbing experiences can be erased, and experiences can be shaped to your benefit. *Didn't get to summer in Biarritz?* Invent the experience! *Implant it! Shape* your operating system!

FREE YOURSELF OF TRAGEDY!
FREE YOURSELF OF ANGUISH!
BE HAPPY NOW!

Tired of the endless process of forging narratives on social media? With digito-neural surgery, experiences *become* real! Experiences are *made* real! Not only will others believe it, but you will too! The virtual is the real because the real *is* virtual.

REWRITE YOUR SELF!
REWIRE YOUR SELF FOR *HAPPINESS!*
NO MEDICATION REQUIRED!
AND NO AWFUL SIDE EFFECTS!

Come to Candid, the premiere Digito-Neural Center.
End the biological prejudice once and for all!

DON'T WAIT ANY LONGER!

Get your positive memory implants today! *Get happy today!*

DON'T BE LEFT BEHIND –
JOIN THE HUMANO-DIGITIST FUTURE!

CALL
1-800-DIGITO-BLISS
NOW!

HURRICANE BAUBO

IT COMMENCED WITH A STRANGE, striking silence, as if all sonic elements had been briefly and swiftly sucked out of the air, then returned, hitting the atmosphere like a bold exclamation mark, starting in one city, proliferating in others, manifesting in every state, like a tropical cyclone, a shockwave reverberating throughout the world, striking one country, then another, erupting in continent after continent, tearing through the globe, until the entire surveillance network of the planetary sphere was in tumult, though it wasn't an act of natural randomness.

The agents monitoring surveillance systems first noticed several masked figures entering the field of vision of their cameras, in seemingly chaotic patterns, enacting odd gestures, portending extreme fury surrounding an eerily calm & hollowed-out eye.

As they placed what resembled radios in different parts of the public square, then began a series of shifting, apparently choreographed movements, police thought they were performance artists engaging in guerilla street theater.

From time to time, the officers observed their actions, with no serious concern, yet, when they went to the devices they had distributed about the area and manipulated the dials on their machines, carefully tuning them back & forth, shifting between static, co-channel, radio transmitter, or electrical interference and clear signals, as if searching not for radio stations, but *between* them, the abrupt, bewildering total absence of sound baffled the officers.

At first, the agents thought their audio channels went dead, or that there was an act of sabotage in effect, but after investigating the signals, no technical defect was evident, and the marked, prominent sonic presence of silence defied the probability of any audio failure. The only existing sound seemed to be the low pulse of the cosmos itself, galactic radio noise, as if nothing but sun flares & solar wind were audible and magnified.

When a single odd sound erupted with extreme violent force through their channels, a sound that seemed to resemble two cunctated — or elongated, it couldn't be differentiated — letters immediately before the return of general atmospherics, the agents believed something was amiss.

With the inexplicable events occurring throughout the world, all further deviations of reality, however minute, gave rise to extreme paranoia, to a disquieting & distracting alertness, a readiness for further such deviations, but one never knew when and where they would occur. When however surveillance systems detected the presence of a possible terrorist, the agents shifted focus to the suspect.

Moving between dome, bullet, PTZ, and all end-to-end surveillance, they tracked him, tilting up, down, zooming closer & far away, following him as he moved, checking video surveillance in domain awareness and real-time crime centers, as well as public & private video feeds.

Through their Control Center, the police are everywhere and they see and hear everything – every breath you take, and every move you make, every step you take, their eyes have seen you stand in your door, their eyes have seen you, free from disguise, their eyes have seen you, walking through a city under surveillance eyes — every single day, and every word you say, they are watching you — let them photograph your soul, memorize your movements on an endless scroll — can't you see, you belong to them? They'll be watching you —

While determining the spatial distance between the eyes, the length of the nose, and the chin shape of the suspect, converting the information to greyscale and searching image databases to match existing face templates, alarms were raised on other monitors before the agents. The system detected another terrorist, then another, and yet more.

Clicking on the map, Control Center brings up relevant cameras, checking Network Distributed Architecture, Remote Monitoring, and Wide Area Surveillance, as they listen to everything, engaging additional surveillance cameras and video recorders. The eye in the sky watching us all, the eye in the sky watching everything, hearing everything, recording everything; yet it doesn't only intake, it extends outward, entering the bodies it observes, taking them over, exploring them, breaking them down, rearranging them, a digital mechanics of power seizing control of bodies, sculpting them with techniques whose speed and efficiency are dizzying, producing subjected and docile citizens — high fidelity two-way audio devices transmit broadcasts:

"We record and protect. Safe is a wonderful feeling.
We record and protect."

As the police work to trace the suspects, more and more terrorists begin to appear, setting off further monitor alarms, with every street, alley, square, and park proliferating with them, as if a conference of terrorists is in effect, & the sound of ammunition is heard, 50-cartridge box magazine clips clicking into chambers, flares striking, Molotov cocktails exploding, radio signals crackling, setting off every single monitor alarm: — cameras tilting, zooming, measuring, detecting, an infinite barrage of faces flitting thru databases at incomprehensible velocities, a tsunami of terrorists amassing, testing the limits of the agents' ability to monitor the system, testing the endurance of the systems' processors, whose temperatures begin to swiftly increase, panic intensifying, nerves splintering.

In the midst of reviewing surveillance footage, rewinding material to trace the incoming presence and pathways of the terrorists, several agents discover that, through strategic locations, the performance artists projected images that locked onto and secured to each face in the crowd, digitally layering the face of a known terrorist over every individual, turning every citizen into a terrorist, pushing the surveillance system to its near-breaking point.

The recording of terrorist noises clicks off. The projected images fade out. Every terrorist becomes a citizen. Horns begin to sound, batons are clacked against street posts, second-line beats are thundered out, polyrhythms in marching cadences, shuffle and press rolls, the sharp, invigorating punctuation of congas, repiniques, agogôs, cuícas and other percussion, provoking the masked figures to begin dancing lewdly, wildly, disrupting the indiscriminate flow of the crowd, which begins to gather round and observe them, transfixed by their feral actions.

When the women lift their skirts, the sound of the two cunctated letters bursts forth again with violent force

haaaaaa
haaaaaaa
haaaaaaa

piercing the two-way audio devices as the women exhibit their vulvas, which they make up into faces, their genitals transformed into masks that, through their grimacing, become bursts of laughter, wild explosions of raucous, maniacal laughter that coincide with the amplified sound of infinitely looping laughter repeating from the Lachsacks dispersing throughout the piazza.

Zooming in closer to gaze at the exposed organs of the women's bodies, the police direct all cameras toward their crotches, & as they are gazing at their fucking cunts, they see shiny, glass-like balls inside of them out of which, unexpectedly, high-powered laser beams burst forth, projecting from them with piercing force, degrading, blinding, damaging, and destroying the lenses of all of the cameras.

Surveillance disrupted; invasive tactics short-circuited.

The women walk off, dispersing in different directions, moving to the edges, the borders, the peripheries of the city: to docks, to coastlines, to edges and extremities where water opens other pathways, moving outside the bounded confines of land.

The extreme upward motion of their eyewall sends density ripples through the tropopause.

MAP THE UNIVERSE, MAP THE UNCONSCIOUS

TO THE DIGITO-HUMANISTS, EVENTUALLY — it was only a matter of time —, the entire universe would be measured and mapped, and the all-powerful syndicates and silicon valley utopians would position cameras everywhere, with near, far, and even distant galaxies being overlaid with a system of encompassing grids, then networked, tracked, documented, recorded, mined. Further, they believed that everything would eventually be known, that even the unconscious would be eliminated, that all mysteries would be solved, for no substantive reason exists for enigmas to persist, it is only a matter of technique, and so, imaginably, a hyperconscious super-consciousness could be developed where nothing would be hidden, nothing would be forgotten, & everything would be known. It is a mere mechanical exercise, like extracting oil from the depths of the earth, excavating diamond mines, or extricating pearls from oyster nacres.

Extract everything! Frack your brain!! they proclaimed with neurological glee. Unearth the unconscious, make it entirely accessible, traceable, manipulable: *upload it, access it, utilize it!* Once we create a digital map of your unconscious, you can access it just like computer files — never forget; always remember! With the extraction of your unconscious, you can have eternal, permanent memory. Don't suffer from slips of the tongue any longer! Be free of unconscious symptoms! Unite the id, the ego, & the super-ego! Enter into your most private thoughts and concerns and extract them! Release repressed traumas and free yourself of all psychic ailments! Don't be dominated any longer by parasitic hosts and unconscious representations — gain total control of your self. Become aware of all past representations, of their presence and activity, for they are active in you. Free the lasting associations of perceptions that below the threshold of consciousness are actively in conflict with each other. Don't let yourself be possessed! Don't be tyrannized by shadow systems that will bring you to your ruin. Such are the roots of antipathies, suspicions, perversions, and so on, all of which our dream systems betray. The life path of the hysterical and the melancholic is paved with shadow systems. Free yourselves of *idées fixes*; free yourself of hysterical symptoms! Hysterical access is nothing but the explosion of an *idée fixe*. Unconscious psychic dynamism is nothing more than a teratoid — discard all outmoded scientific conceptions! Daydreams, suppressed emotions, suppressed desires, and the deleterious effects of and various masks taken by frustrated sexual instinct can be eliminated by making everything manifest. *Pure, perfect transparency is within reach!* Although we cannot yet access dark energy and dark matter, we can access the unconscious! Self-deception and unconscious lies can be forever eliminated! Are you farthest from yourself, but a mere cipher of your unconscious? The Socratic dream of self-knowledge is within our grasp! Total self-realization is at hand, they assert, reaffirming the belief in moral and epistemological certainty. Freud, Jung, Maslow, Klein? Meden agan? *Bah!* Self-knowledge isn't a mental process; it's a mechanical one. No more talking cures, no more confessions, no more word association games, no more hypnosis! Primal screams? Don't suffer vague intuitions any longer; make everything manifest! *Extract everything!* Be as clear and as transparent as water. Primary dream contents will be transformed into films. All unconscious primary material will not remain restricted to its own domain; inner perception will no longer be hidden. All instinctual drives and wishes will emerge into consciousness. Eliminate the psychic struggle!

Access the deposit of mankind's whole ancestral experience with the click of a button. *Mechanize the unconscious! Digitize it!* The deposit of all human experience from all of time is at hand. The life of the individual no longer has to be determined in invisible ways. All reactions and aptitudes can be made conscious. Free will reigns again; the hegemony of reason returns! Do not fear somnambulic influences; do not fear the residues that would remain in the depths of the psyche. Unveil the god! *Strip Isis of her dress!* Activate the instincts; utilize the instincts; *monetize the instincts!* Liberate the unconscious! Give rise to dynamic affects! Unleash the subwaking self! *Now!* Descend into the image-producing abyss!

OPERATION
WORDSTORM

TIMES SQUARE, *and all main commercial mega-centers of the world*. Night. — Immense images flit forth on the building's 7,000 + ft² three-dimensional LED video screens, jettisoned across their smooth surfaces of 10 million pixels at eye-searing velocity: pre-fabricated ads and real-time mixes of pre-constructed content fuse with live images from the buildings environs, a blitzkrieg of 280 trillion colors of commerce and ad agency lingo assaulting the nerves with their hollow, pithy, inclusive, pacifying gaiety. — *A piece of paper is dropped from the sky.* — Absorbing external input, the screens adopt affects from the surrounding environment and project them anew as their own, fusing screens with crowd, crowd with screens, adopting all topical concerns of the day:——:integrative, unitary capitalism whose flow is never interrupted, for it absorbs *&* regurgitates everything in its path. If it is grey and rainy, the sign's mood, color tone, and message change to contrast the dreariness with eternal optimism. — Someone picks up the fallen paper, reads it: *I saw that everyone in the world was doomed to happiness.* — Corporate slogans manifest and disappear across the screens like the innocuous, jejune imagery of slot machines. A series of poetic phrases, at first unnoticed, disrupt the placid, ingratiating tone of "the temple where vision gets built": Empowering communities: 261,000 People empowered digitally + financially. — *Farewell until eternity, where you and I shall not find ourselves together.* — Connecting around the world. — *Not knowing how to express myself without pagan words, I'd rather remain silent.* — Representing commitment to innovation, visualizing the latest financial data in real-time:

Latest Value: 6.269.73% Change +0.13% As of 2:10 P.M., July 21 — *I turned silences and nights into words. What was unutterable, I wrote down. I made the whirling world stand still.* — The best is yet to come. — When the unending electro-fiber optick streams and currents of water that flow out of and into the company's stately logo morph into streams of oil and images of flared *&* vented natural gas burst forth from its body to the accompanying sonic noise of such events, pedestrian and vehicular traffic is disrupted. — *Another piece of paper is dropped from the sky.* — After the pacific, congenial music of the screen cuts to silence then erupts into a flotilla of foghorns, batteries of artillery guns, factory sirens, and steam whistle machines screeching out 'The Internationale' and 'La Marseillaise,' all traffic comes to a standstill. — The melodies of this incursion drift far beyond the commercial center, sounding in the distant, north and south, extending in multiple directions, vertically, horizontally, transversally. — Images of contaminated surface *&* groundwater surge across the screens, intercut with films of erosion, ground disturbances, chemical spills, the migration of underground gases *&* resulting explosions, fires, emission of carcinogenic chemicals. — Someone picks up the fallen paper, reads it: *I am nothing. I will never be anything. I cannot want to be anything. Apart from that, I carry within me all the dreams of the world.* — The security dept. is enacted. Cameras are set in motion, scanning the vicinity above, below, around, north, south, east, west for suspects. The screens cannot be secured or recovered; they continue to proliferate alien imagery, an abundance of flowers, winding and intertwining, constantly growing and changing forms and colors in exotic luxuriance, sprouting out of one another. — More pieces of paper are dropped from the sky, a voluminous number of them, falling around the surrounding buildings like confetti, but it is not New Year's Eve. — Gazing upward, black-clad figures are faintly visible, hovering at the edges of buildings, perched on corners, crossing frontiers, transgressing boundaries, as if set to jump, to leap down, to — *attack? assassinate? annihilate?* They hold position, still as stones, gazing at the world below, interrupting its flow, altering angles of guided perception, transfixing certain passersby. Terrorists? Freedom fighters? Punk rockers? Anarchists? — Scenes from the surrounding streets flicker across the screens; every citizen becomes a suspect; eyes turn on other eyes; surveillance extends from person to person; a network of individual agents of surveillance: control has been internalized, cut into the nerves, made cellular, altered the organs. — People pick up the fallen pieces of paper: *The form of a city changes faster, alas! than a mortal's heart.* — The figures perched atop the surrounding buildings slowly open & close umbrellas, as do the figures on the street. Some people flee them in panic; others are immobilized, or stand in rapt awe before them. — All signage in the center goes dark, disrupting the thousand angles of the multi-directional spectacle, save for the building's 7,000+ ft² screens, across which flit images of war intercut with extreme pornographic scenes, bondage, domination, sadism, animals tearing prey to pieces — economic flows are disrupted, diverted, breaking the smooth stream of turbulent capital. — The black-clad figures emerge from and move in random directions toward civilians in the street: east, north, west, south, vertically, horizontally, transversally: some carrying long black pipes, others black umbrellas from which lasers shoot upwards and in various directions, piercing every camera lens in the area, blinding and shattering them. — The screens go blank, are voided out, blackened. — The sound of foghorns, firing guns, sirens, and steam whistles fade out to stark silence. — Every suspect becomes a citizen. — The figures atop the surrounding buildings hold up shifting placards upon which they have scrawled passages: *It is not to a utopian "state of nature" to which I aspire but to a real "spirit of nature," surpassing the pure intellectual speculation of the interpretation of the world to finally live fully; to become and to be because I am that that I am without perhaps never knowing it.* — Emergency alarms sound in the distance; sirens screech like terrified birds; highly impulsive vibrations are set off in the air by the violent blade slapping of helicopter rotors. — More pieces of paper are dropped from the sky, slowly drifting to the ground, falling like feathers, breaking currents of time & space. Some people observe their pathways, wander after them, unknowingly disrupting patterned lines of circulation, crossing streets at oblong angles to seek out the landing sites of the falling paper. — Deauthentication attacks disable all cellphones & networks in the area.

Traffic lights go dark, street lights go dark, building lights go dark.

The chaotic images' hold on the mind and body is broken; the sensorium commune begins to loosen and grow more receptive. —

Now in close proximity to every citizen, the figures on the street raise their long black pipes to peoples' ears & whisper into them in the many languages of the earth, moving from person to person to person, word spreading from body to body, carried by breath, carried by oxygen, entering the ear, the logos putting flesh into metamorphosis:

Companions in pathos, who barely murmur, go with your lamp spent & return the jewels. A new mystery sings in your bones. Cultivate your legitimate strangeness. —

The figures lower their pipes and walk away: horizontally, vertically, transversally, seemingly almost evaporating like mist, drifting off into unexpected currents, points, and vortexes of the psycho-geo-graphical reliefs of the city as the spectators are left with their words, some internalizing them, some rejecting them, some seeking to embody them, some carrying the verse in silence, broken into states of question, broken into states of musing, provoking them to disorder entry-exit zones, departing from entries, entering from exits, pursuing only contours of personal affect, æsthetic juxtaposition, and spontaneous encounter or psychic association.

The voices of the world becoming quieter and fewer, some citizens remain stock still, poised like rocks, rooted as if in absolute nature, standing before a placard left behind by the black-clad figures, ruminating its enigmas:

> There is neither something nor nothing: this terrible contradiction constitutes the height of skepticism. The last bit of ground is slipping away from under our feet; the end of the whole is no longer "nothing," but something more terrible, even more inconceivable, formless, monstrous, black — and resplendent with a celestial brilliance. — The core of the world, we call it "Black Radiance," "Black Illusion."

VIRTUAL REALITY TANK

Live out the experiences you desire but never thought you could or would have!

Can't fly to the moon, can't travel to Monaco or Nice? Movie star won't respond to your DMs? Come to the Virtual Reality Tank & live the experience as you never would have, *even if you were actually there!*

Don't be subject to imperfect vacations; don't be subject to dilemmas of any kind. Tired of waiting in airports? Tired of standing in lines? Tired of bad food and grumpy waiters? Tired of people you don't feel comfortable with, or just don't like?

Perfect and shape life as you desire!

DON'T BE LIMITED BY REALITY!

CANCEL ALL IMPERFECTIONS!

CANCEL ALL FLAWS!!

The Virtual Reality Tank (VRT), where life is more real than life! Where life is *hyperreal!* Experience it now! Experience *anything* now! Experience *everything* now!

The VRT, where dreams are made real, and experiences are remembered as if they actually happened! Remember everything in perfect detail!

WHY BE REAL
WHEN YOU CAN BE
HYPERREAL?

ENHANCE REALITY

at the VRT

It's like supercharging your computer!

DIGITIZE LIFE! *DIGITIZE EXPERIENCE!*

INDIVIDUAL AND GROUP EXPERIENCES AVAILABLE!

DON'T LET REALITY CONTROL YOU

MAKE THE LIFE *YOU* DESIRE!

VIRTUALIZE YOUR SOUL!

VIRTUALIZE LIFE!

AIR

SHE HAD BEEN COLLECTING FEATHERS for some time, finding one after another in her meandering throughout the world, though not with any particular intent. She was struck by them, and when an occasion arose, she tended to it, attuned as she was to happenstance, to being captured by objects, sensitive to the force and power of fleeting, subtle things, to their effect upon her nerves, and their latent, subterranean potentialities. It was as if opening to them, being receptive to their presence, almost made them manifest more regularly, or made her more aware of their presence in the world. Each feather, even if of the same bird, even if ostensibly similar, was distinct, as particular and discrete as individual leaves, and she accumulated more and more of them over time, placing them in a box in her studio. Often, she would examine them, studying the calami, the rachis, and the barbs and barbules of each, noticing that their intricate, microscopic hooks interlocked to create flat vanes or contour feathers that gave definition to the form of the body of the bird and functioned as aerodynamic devices. A host of the feathers were remiges, others rectrices, others coverts or semiplumes, each of whose microstructures differed, giving them their particular character. There were an abundance which, while being mainly remiges or rectrices, & being structured just like other feathers, hailed from some bird unknown to her, a rare, clearly quite large one, perhaps from the Andes, if not elsewhere.

The feathers struck her as being those of an elusive species yet, one day, she came upon a bevy of them, as if an entire flock had been plucked, or all of them shed their feathers just prior to death, or transformation, like a snake divesting itself of its skin.

But she didn't think such a rare bird would organize into a flock, or that their molting process would occur simultaneously, or that they would congregate in a city. The profusion of feathers was startling, for she had never come across more than two or three at once, of any bird, and many of these feathers were stained a dark reddish color, their calami and rami ruptured, or mutilated, intimating that they had suffered some kind of violence. Had they been flying overhead and struck by the fan blades of a plane?

At first, she didn't know if the feathers were in fact stained, or only absorbing light from the intensity of the flashing clocks that ticked and sounded everywhere in the city, marking space like a grid of garish road signs crisscrossing the sky. The texture and density of their barbs were different too from those of all of the other feathers that she had collected. In analyzing them, she deduced the bird to be one that was largely quiet, or silent, but which moved with startling velocity. Whether that was accurate or not, when she returned home and examined the feathers with more care, the reddish hue was not absorbed light, but blood, the traces of which she let remain as the final marker of the life of the bird.

After placing the feathers in a separate box on a high shelf next to another box of feathers in her studio, she climbed down the ladder and, when folding it up, clipped the edge of the boxes, both of which tumbled off the shelf and opened.

Putting the ladder against the wall, she sat & watched the feathers falling, gusted by the wind coming through her windows, skittering here and there, at different speeds, until, one by one, they eventually touched ground, resting there, but still moving, the breeze buffeting them about, pitching them gently back and forth, like the blades of a rocking chair altering the center of gravity.

Following the arc of one of the descending objects, she tried to determine its pathway, tracing its haphazard movement through the air. When she reached out to seize it, the feather eluded her grasp — a light gust of wind sent it whooshing from her fingers. She watched as it skittered across the floor.

Absorbed in thought before the play of the wind, the idea for an installation was born in her and she began to conceive of how it would be constructed.

One at a time, in a large, expansive space, to the accompaniment of the sound of a plane landing and taking off, a feather would fall from a different opening in the ceiling and, using shifting currents of air emerging from myriad directions, erupting at different points throughout space, at varying speeds, each changing, each unpredictable, occurring truly at random, with no discernible pattern, the feather would be buffeted here and there until, eventually, it reached the ground, unless it could be grasped by whoever encountered it. One person alone would be permitted to enter the space every hour, but with no guarantee that a feather would ever manifest. If it did, and it reached the ground, it would be retrieved and destroyed, lost forever. Sometimes, it would be pulled swiftly downward with a vacuum force, toward a series of continuously shifting openings in the floor. As at the site where she found the bevy of odd feathers, a digital atomic clock face would flash and tick and sound thru-out the room, marking time like a sentinel. With each lost feather, an additional clock face would appear on the wall, increasing and intensifying the flashing, ticking, & sounding, whereas when a feather could be seized, the clocks would vanish, go silent, and the blinds on all of the windows would open instantaneously, flooding the room with the sudden illumination of sunlight bursting through it, or the sudden illumination of the gelid blue flash of a lightning bolt, accompanied by its percussive, thunderous crack. Once all of the feathers that she had collected had fallen, the installation would be terminated & never repeated.

She called the work AIR, and when it opened, person after person entered the space one at a time, wandering through it, at first attentive, trembling with anticipation, alert, awake to the potentiality of the event, but as they traversed the installation, with no immediate, palpable action and their relation to the space and the subtle unfoldings of the event eluding them, they took out their smartphones and began scanning the ceiling, searching for the place from where the feather would fall, but to no avail. Photographing the space wasn't of much interest since the walls, floor, and ceiling were entirely bare, save for the flashing atomic digital clock face, prompting most people to take image after image of themselves, each of which they examined in close detail, enlarging them, zooming in on various parts of their faces, altering this, altering that, perfecting their representations with filters, engrossed by the depiction of themselves and the infinite manifestations of their simulacra, proliferating as they did without reserve, cubed to near-infinity, a virtual gallery of interminable copies, a hall of mirrors replicating the self ad nauseam.

Losing perceptive acumen, boredom seething, the senses going slack, since most personal social media sites had been dismantled, short-circuited, or corrupted, the spectators began aimlessly surfing the internet, or chatting with whoever might be around, babbling relentlessly, words but noise, in the space in which they perceived nothing — *There's nothing here; no, it's an empty space, just a clock* —, hardly aware even of how their voice changed in the space, or how the space changed their voice, disembodied from the space, absent from the present, absent from the subtle alterations in reality, the feather falling from the ceiling unbeknownst to them, the flashes of the digital clock face getting subtly brighter, the flashes more intense, gentle wind currents coursing through the room as they gazed at their images in their phones, looking on their screens more at how they looked to others during video calls than being in real dialogue, uploading pictures to their data storage spaces, emailing pictures of themselves to their friends and families, the feather concluding its trajectory, the feather drawn into an opening in the ground, destroyed, lost forever, a further clock face appearing on the wall, clocks flashing, ticking, sounding with greater intensity, each tick, each tock, compounded one upon another, as they remained enraptured by their smart-phones, then left the space, the hour concluded, and, according to them, nothing in particular ever happening.

Eventually, with more and more feathers being destroyed, lost forever, the clock faces multiplied exponentially, as did their flashing LED lights, and over time, people entered the installation not to encounter the feather & to attempt to grasp it, but because they were bewitched by the lights, and some people actually wanted the feather to be destroyed and, lost in the play of flashing lights in the room and upon the feather, the hue of blood invisible to them due to its being mixed or intensified by the color of the LED lights, not truly present but lost in the glittering marvel, they watched the feather descend, watched it buffeted by the wind, watched it painted with light, and recorded the death of the feather, privileging their act of documenting the moment over being present in it, savoring the spectacular representation of reality over their interplay with it, with the event that can open a horizon.

Others, held in thrall by the precision of the atomic clock faces and their proliferating noises, a precision and noise that effaced the moment, were entirely oblivious to the feather & kept marking time, trying to count even milliseconds. Still others took drugs to enhance and intensify their experience, seemingly their perception, but, captivated by minutiae, astray in the ecstasy of the information of perception, they were severed from the lucid clarity of the senses, from moods and atmospheres, and in the dazzlement of the phantasmagoric iridescence of colors and sounds, the feather moved through space with the whimsicality of a soap bubble, their cognition slow and laborious, enfolded in a lethargic process of documentation as if in an enveloping membrane, instead of in perceiving and responding, entranced by the movement of the falling feather and the breezes buffeting it about, they were stilled into non-action, into a kind of catatonic stupor, until the last person entered the room and the last feather fell and was destroyed, lost forever, and the entire room was covered in atomic digital clock faces and time was compounded, intensified, echoing, beat upon beat: millisecond, second, minute, hour hands sounding one over the other, a thick, impenetrable density of time, like a pool filled with sand, ticking away at microwave frequencies, temporality now universal, cesiumic, only nanoseconds from total absolute cosmic precision, the flashing lights increasing layer by layer, until the room became a dense web of layered light, filling every square inch of the space, as if light was air — soon, the oxygen was sucked out of the air tight installation, making it a space no one could enter, except with a spacesuit or an oxygen tank, and AIR became a new work, which she called AR, with the lack of oxygen and intensity of light and sound creating a total loss of bearing and navigability.

OPERATION
TRADEWINDS

16 SEPTEMBER: Wall Street, NYC, The New York Stock Exchange, the vibrating center of capitalism, and the trading stock floor, the bourse, the marketplace, *of every major country in the world.* —

The ceremonial bell rings, the market opens in the Yankee Stadium of finance, and elsewhere around the world, upon the arrival of each opening hour in time zone after time zone, till, from west to east, the entire world is a buzzing marketplace. The pulse and the heartbeat of capitalism throb with bristling intensity across latitude and longitude, like jet streams swiftly pushing weather systems west to east in unbroken zonal flows. A banner hangs from the ceiling:

NEW YORK STOCK EXCHANGE
The world puts its stock in us.

Letters, arrows, numbers indicate price & volume, ticker signs flash on and off, an esoteric symbol system of shares traded (in the ks, Ms, Bs), prices traded, change directions, change amounts flickering across screens like horse names at race tracks, or destination and arrival data on train station split-flap displays, but with blistering velocity. *Price patterns = human behavior in price form.* A spectrum of red, green, blue, and white colors indicate trading character, illuminating the room with their hues, like a simplified kaleidoscope or economic funhouse where all is stripped to bare fact. Quotes continuously scroll across screens of financial channels and wires, displaying current or just slightly delayed data. — *When that first storm been here, when that first storm been here, I don't think you been born.* —— Amidst the bustle, mania, and chaos, none of the floor traders heard that first aural sotto voce incursion sounding through the speakers, & when lower trading stocks were displayed on the ticker instead of higher ones, it was only a technical snafu that seemed to be in effect yet, when stock letters, arrows, and numbers began to display startlingly high & negative values, symbols pointed in nonsensical directions, spinning even counterclockwise, like whimsical carnival targets, & trading character colors bled into other indiscernible hues, giving no clear indication of market events, panic began to set in, disrupting the smooth, rapid flow of capital. ——

Screens are shut down to reset; trading ceases; the flow of the current is broken.

A nervous silence seethes beneath quiet anxious murmurs. Dead air pervades the room: an uncanny forbearing from speech.

Minutes pass—long, slow, interminable minutes that elongate time, making it seem like eons unfold—fingers drummed, nails bit, hairs torn from supraorbital ridges, shirts, pants, ties readjusted, nerves torched, balls clutched, scratched, squeezed until, finally, screens reload, numbers light up the space like fireworks, ticker symbols flicker back on, economic gaiety returns: *sell, buy, sell, buy, buy, buy! sell, sell, sell!* ——

In the mad din, a voice calls out: "Once, twice. Once, twice." "Another cent." "Thank ye, gentlemen," but no one can discern if it is a recording, the live voice of a trader, or the interjection of an interloper. The floor is a hurricane of shouting voices yet, at 12:01 P.M., to the astonishment of everyone in the room, the opening and closing bell sounds again, but instead of being struck 9 times, it is struck continually, sounding a stately 16-bar theme in B♭ Lydian mode, a dynamic, energetic processional march. The entire room turns toward the podium and, to their disbelief, they see the figure of Mickey Mouse clapping, gesturing, saluting, pointing, nodding his smiling juvenile head, blinking innocuous happy happy eyes, waving & giving the thumbs up, which at first amuses everyone, but it troubles them too, particularly when the cartoon figure starts to sing, but more because the bell only sounds at the opening and closing of the day. — *And that first storm*, the mouse incanted in a deep, heavy contralto, gesturing toward the floor below, *you know about earthquake? You know about dark night? I ain't afraid 'bout a dark night now.* —

As traders react in shock, yelling, shouting, fuming amongst themselves while hurling curses at the mascot, at numerous points throughout the trading floors, immense sluices open through which tons of coffee grinds rush inward, a seemingly endless, wild, turbulent flow of grinds whose noise is frightening, flooding the entire floor at startling speeds, a veritable chaos of grinds, a tsunami of goods, swiftly burying the traders & others up to their hips as they make frantic phone calls, setting security in motion, informing CEOs, informing police, but all motion proves difficult. — *I had to walk on my hand and knee, Mickey continues singing, because the world going upside down… I been through all them thing.* — Nearly immobile, save for their arms and heads, the traders gaze up to see the cartoon mascot remove its head and, upon being joined by a cluster of black men & women, all of whom stand behind her, she starts singing:

> **There was much tension at Knip**
> **The slaves have decided today,**
> **Things will end.**
> **Slaves have decided today:**
> **Liberty will start**
> **When the bell sounds …**

As the last line was sung, the woman in the Mickey Mouse costume went silent, & a disturbed hush pervaded the stock exchange, as if most of the sound had been sucked out of the room.

From the back of the cluster, a group of female slaves walk boldly forward, taking the front line. Some bear iron muzzles infused with copper in-lays that surround their heads, faces, and mouths. Clamped around the neck like a collar, the device drives up and across their faces, arching around their noses and eyes. Between the iron bars framing their noses are circular pieces of iron that continue past their foreheads and clasp against their heads, where the frame connects back with the locked collar. The mouthpiece of the muzzle rests against their lips while others run along the inner gum lines of their teeth. A flat plate continuously presses down on their tongues, preventing them from speaking or singing.

Others bear 50-pound iron horns, heavy, cumbersome neck contraptions several feet in height, with 2'4" & 6' cross pieces from which hang little bells. Chains fastened around their necks are secured with locking iron pins at the nape. The iron horns exert such weight upon the neck & shoulders of the slaves that they create deep cuts & sores, scarring the women. Blood trickles down their collarbones, over their breasts, onto the floor.

The female slaves stare fiercely at the traders below, & in the silence, the iron horned slaves sway gently back & forth, the tinkling bells of the restraints mingling with the subdued clacking of stock letters, arrows, ticking numbers — market values rising, plummeting, their colors all shifting to white, flickering across the dark flesh of the slaves. The hallowed banner goes up in a burst of flames; a new one drops from the ceiling:

NEW YORK STOCK EXCHANGE

We put the world in our stocks & bonds.

The bodies of black men, women, and children drop from the ceiling: *THUD, THUD, THUD, THUD, THUD,* swinging from ropes over the traders.

Mickey steps forward and, joined by the cluster of black men and women, all begin singing in unison while the data of stock prices & volumes continue recounting values:

Jump down, turn around & pick a bale of cotton.
Jump down, turn around & pick a bale a day.

Oh Lordy, pick a bale of cotton,
Oh Lordy, pick a bale a day.

The singing is so loud and, in such haunting tones, that the traders can barely endure it. It sounds like an animal crying to its young.

Despite sticking their fingers deep in their ears, the singing is so intense & so strident that it penetrates to the depths of the traders' eardrums—they twist and turn in the coffee grinds, making violent torsions, squirming like maggots in cheese.

Northern trees, Mickey interjects, *bear a strange fruit,*
Blood on the leaves and blood at the root,
Black bodies swinging in the northern breeze,
Strange fruit hanging from the buttonwood tree…

When the final tone of the word *tree* eventually fades out, the muzzled and crossed slaves step forward again and stare out in silence, peering at the traders, peering around the room, which creaks with the sound of straining ropes, ticking stock prices, tinkling bells, and another turbulent influx of coffee grinds rushing inward with storm-like vehemence, burying the traders up to their shoulders.

Concluding their silence, on the downbeat, the cluster of men and women break into song again, their voices still loud and strident:

That nigger from Shiloh can pick a bale of cotton
That nigger from Shiloh can pick a day.
Takes a might big man to pick a bale of cotton
Takes a might big man to pick a day.

Me & my wife gonna pick a bale of cotton,
Me & my wife gonna pick a bale a day.

Stressed to snapping point, the ropes crack, give way —
black bodies drop from the sky, one after another: men, women,
children, each plunging like bloodied & bludgeoned weights
into the coffee grinds, falling amongst the traders: limbs turning, twisting, bending, some falling head first into the goods:
their feet sticking out of the brown grinds; others falling feet
first into them: their scarred heads sticking out of the brown
grinds; others falling at twisted angles, bodies contorted:
elbows, knees, shoulders sticking out of the brown grinds,
lashed backs curving above the brown grinds: crisscrossed lati-
tudinal and longitudinal lines, diagonal lines, blood lines, like
disrupting Coriolis forces setting streams adrift. The topography of the slave; the topography of economy; the topography
of capitalism————————X

Sluices open in the ceiling and, like snow, gentle puffs of
cotton fall from each, one after another, drifting slowly downward till they land delicately upon the coffee grinds, surrounding the heads of the traders, who try to blow the balls of cotton
away from their mouths, but after the cotton balls roll forward,
they fall back, tumbling against their mouths, forcing them
to breath in the toil, sweat, and blood contained in the goods.

The spectrum of colors indicating the trading character of
stocks & bonds all turn red. The room glows with burning hot
hues — the cotton illuminated by the dark crimson pigment of
economy.

Stepping forward, the black woman in the Mickey Mouse costume sets off the bell again, and the chorus sings with her as she tosses stick after stick of toy dynamite onto the trading floor, each punctuated with a shout:

Tambú player come with me
To Porto Marie!
Come with me to
Niger Hill!
Barricade at Niger Hill!
Liberty for everybody!
Break the bell to stop it from
Sounding.
Oh mama, rebellion at
Bandabou!
Men in rebellion,
Rebellion at Bandabou.
Women also in fight.
Break the bell to stop it from
Sounding.
Break the bell...

Climbing down from the podium, the male and female slaves begin to dismantle the bell, taking it apart piece by piece, stripping it of its clapper and other elements, ridding each other of muzzles, clasps, and crosses, too, until they are entirely free of all encumbrances, each exulting over their emancipation.

After starting a fire on the podium, they turn the stock exchange bell over & begin a ceremonial feast to celebrate their freedom, cooking pot after pot of Hop'n johns in the bell-bowl as the traders are entirely immobilized in coffee grinds, even their arms completely buried in the goods, with them nothing but a series of white heads nervously twitching back & forth across the trading floor like sematic signals on a dark sea.

When food has been cooked for everyone, the liberated men and women use the bells from the iron crosses as little bowls, filling them all, and feeding each of the traders, jubilating in song as they distribute the food and then feed themselves, their bodies no longer devices of torture, but instruments out of which music is born, instruments generating commentary, exaltations, lamentations, invocations, and good tidings:

Ain't gonna put me in no stockade no more,
Ain't gonna put me in no bond no more,

Picking up sticks, the men and women form a circle, dancing and jumping to rhythms beat by the tambú drummer and the array of heru players clanging tres pidas, dos pidas, triangels, wiris, and chapis, clanging out faster and more intense rhythms, the heru and bari players in $^{12}/_8$, the lead singer in $^4/_4$, the cluster of men and women clapping, stomping, using their bodies as percussion too, shifting between different time signatures, creating complex polyrhythms as others from the cluster join in the song:

No more stocks, no more bonds,
We done broke the clock, we done broke the bell,
Gonna build ourselves a nouveau monde,
That's right, you know it be so,
Gonna build ourselves a nouveau monde...
Ain't gonna stock me in no more,
Ain't gonna bond me up no more...
We gonna burn the world's stocks and bonds,
We gonna burn...

Round and round they go, their movements becoming livelier with each circular procession, knees bent, fists closed, forearms upright, moving forward on prancing feet, limbs

95

convulsive, shaking, till the percussionists beat and clang out even more intense rhythms, leading to an explosive crescendo, the performance ending with fierce, jubilant shouts.

Having concluded their song, the freed men and women excise the Buttonwood Agreement from behind its bulletproof glass, hold it up before the heads of the traders, and incinerate it on the podium, name after name burned away, becoming nothing but ash, indistinguishable amongst the ocean of coffee grinds..........

The letters, arrows, and numbers indicating stock names, prices, & volume all go berserk — arrows pointing downward, values plummeting to high negatives, traded shares gone to zero, Advisor Group Holdings 'F'; Outlook? .... *Destabilized* ~

Stock name after stock name disappear from screens in a blinding flurry, like figures rushing together on a roulette wheel, each and every screen erupting into a chaos of indiscernible letters and numbers; each and every ticker eventually going blank, ending in the total erasure of the market, the heads of the traders violently rocking back and forth, twitching spasmodically, their eyes opening and closing before the empty screens, flickering vehemently, as if struggling to fight off hallucinations, but the voided market remains, an abyss has been opened up, a hall of black screens usurping the mad din of economy after which, one by one, at a slow, measured pace, the names of slaves begin to appear on the ticker boards, not however listed, as the stocks, in descending hierarchical order, but in circular fashion, in and out, beginning like the four cardinal points of the compass, right opposite to each other, and so continuing until the screens are filled, one after another, a near-infinitely recurring proliferation of slave names, circle after circle of the genealogy of economy ~

OPERATION
SANDBOX

WITH THEIR EXIT PAPERS, every new mother at hospitals around the world received a promotional insert from local banks offering them free beach sets for their children when opening a savings account for them, along with one year of passes for all local beaches or pools. That Friday, from continent to continent, mothers went to their respective banks early in the morning, long before opening hours, to secure the best place in line, only to arrive to find scores of other mothers already queued up, waiting far in advance to secure a premiere spot, some of them having even stayed overnight, and so streets in every village, town, and city around the world were full of mothers, babies in arms, babies swaddled, babies sleeping, babies laughing, babies crying, babies screaming, many of whom could not be pacified, for, what did they know or care about a glistening shiny plastic beach set or free beach passes: — all they wanted was the swollen tit flowing with abundant milk, the ceaseless flow of the machine of the mother producing endless colostrum and being consumed, whether it was clear, white, or yellow did not matter, *just give me that viscous juice, mama*, though some rejected it as rancid & sucked on plastic pacifiers instead, inaugurating their need & desire for plastic from birth, *feed me, feed me, gimme gimme, need, need, need*, while others wailed away and a din of dissonant laughs & cries & screams & rattles sounded thru-out financial institutions around the world as mothers stood in the street like cows fresh from calving, their offspring caterwauling like beasts, flows of women and children, flows of herds and of seed, sperm flows, shit flows, and finally, once again, *menstrual flows*: —— unceasing streams of clear, white, yellow, and red fluids endlessly coursing thru the world, yet despite the existence of nearly 150 million orphans worldwide, all the natalists who professed to love children continued to generate full grown sperm and egg of their own, for like those who generate self-portrait after self-portrait of themselves, they too had an addictive need to reproduce only themselves, to gleefully replicate their family line, ad infinitum, ad nauseam, ad absurdum, ad finem, feeding the algebra of need, succumbing to biological servitude, regardless of the disastrous ecological effects of deforestation, decreased biodiversity, spikes in pollution, spikes in emissions, increased conflicts, pandemics and pandemonium, though rarely ever Pan but instead family as famine-maker of the earth, family as loimos of nature, family as species destroyer, family as bringer of pestilence and plague, family as mortician of the planet.

As the mothers shook their colorful plastic rattles & babbled subhuman nonsensical speech sounds to their offspring, some modest, some freely bearing plump tit to wind, some soiled with miss-shot milk, acid reflux, and drool, some soiled with puke, shit, and piss, startled bank employees began to arrive, dazed by an incongruent amalgam, like something sweet and sour, the stench of waste and baby powder, stupefied by the lines of mothers and children snaking for blocks and blocks up to the doors of their banks which, when opened, were flooded by the near-violent inrush of domestic jugglers clamoring for their beach sets and yearly passes, rattles, bottles, bibs, smartphones in hand, ready to transfer cash, to get their free gifts, to inaugurate their children into the world of exchange.

While the mothers crowded the teller stations, the sound of laughing, crying, screaming babies howling like vile insects was incrementally drowned out by the amplified noise of heavy, rumbling dump trucks and loaders approaching from afar, the tellers bemused by the furious mothers waving, shaking, reiterating the details of the promotional fliers, shaken, physically blown back from their stations as if struck in the chest by violent gusts of wind, or knocked on their feet by the sharp pounding jabs of a boxer—explosive shock waves reverberated through the building as giant holes were bored into the facades of the banks, as if immense wrecking balls had pounded the sides of the buildings, the trucks rushing up, swinging their chutes toward the breaches, their hoppers trembling to breaking point from the vertiginous outflow of sand discharging into the bank, flooding it, fissuring walls, tidal waves of dry, granular mineral particles rising foot by foot thru-out the space, till every person was waist-deep in sand, the particles seeping into wall sockets, crevices, seams, trickling grain by grain into every gap, crack, and opening, entering and clogging computer ports, scratching screens, damaging cooling systems, electronics going dead, lights going dark, the only illumination the round beams of sunlight bursting through the breaches, the banks now giant sandboxes, the children gleefully thrusting their fingers into the grains, grabbing handfuls of them and tossing them in the air, particles of them falling like rain, scintillating in the streams of solar light.

When little currents of water started flowing over the sand, the children grabbed whatever objects were near to them and began making sandcastles, then destroying what they had built, playfully shattering and rebuilding their sand piles again and again, a wanton act of creation and destruction, an outpouring of primal pleasure and delight, shrieking and laughing in the midst of their acts.

And as sand was surging into every bank in the world, their systems had been corrupted, and their branches suffered these uncanny incursions and all been made into playgrounds, an organization of anarchic hackers who called themselves the Modern Prometheans began redistributing the world's total capital to individual bank accounts from continent to continent, and like the destruction of enclosing walls and hedges, it was an opening, a full-scale leveling of the entire world's wealth, flowing ceaselessly from source to source, moving throughout the globe, like milk flowing from a gangrenous tit to the commons, from the Marquesas Islands to Africa, surging as freely and as ceaselessly as the copious tides of shit surged from the anuses of the playing children.

With the coming of noon, the strong beams of sunlight piercing the breaches grew ever more severe in brightness and heat, till the temperature of the sand grew too hot to bear, the light too blinding, an unendurable luminosity.

Removing the diapers of the babies, the stench of shit intensified by the scorching sun, the mothers extracted themselves from the sand, left their waste behind, & upon departing the banks with their offspring, the sound of stone tablets being shattered to pieces echoed 'round them and the morticians of the earth were each handed a book titled *On Procreation* by M.S., which contained the epigraph:

DID I REQUEST THEE, MAKER, FROM MY CLAY
TO MOULD ME MAN? DID I SOLICIT THEE
FROM DARKNESS TO PROMOTE ME?

KNOW YOURSELVES — DO NOT MULTIPLY,
BE INFERTILE, AND LET THE EARTH BE SILENT AFTER YE —
WITH THE DECREASE OF HUMANITY
THE GENERAL HEALTH OF COSMIC LIFE INCREASES ~

OPERATION
DISPORT

OVER TIME, EVERY SQUARE PICA of free space in the world had been usurped by megalithic conglomerates, with advertisements littering the most unsuspected of domains, till no extent of the earth was left unstained and static & digital billboards were as ubiquitous and as pervasive as oxygen, jingles erupting out of every existing aural cavity, tentacular visual, sonic, & psychological assaults, the nervous system, the cellular network, the entire human sensory apparatus infiltrated, invaded, mutated, an all out attack on the psyche and flesh, the battle site of control. Yet, with the continuing subversions of media, social networks, banks, and surveillance systems, conglomerates began to consider more foolproof means of proselytizing. That coupled with their ceaseless need for expansion led them to the outlandish act of shooting holograph digital advertisements toward the earth from strategic locations in space and, dauntingly, to the mounting of illuminated billboards on the moon, the sun deflected from its surface to inhibit its obscuring rays, thus, at nightfall, in every continent in the world, during sleeping hours, like spiders, monkeys, acrobats, and lizards, a clandestine faction of acéphalic figures scaled buildings, cut across highways, slipped into subway stations, penetrated train tunnels, skirted through airports, intruded grandiose halls of commerce, and infiltrated computer systems, setting in motion a tsunami of mutinous incursions that disrupted the colonizing forces of the leviathanic conglomerates.

The attacks began in a blinding light with physical billboards around the world, which were dismantled, set aflame, left burning by roadsides as beacons to the occluded sun. In the vicinity of the fires, strips of partially singed fortune cookie size paper were found that read: *All hail the moon.* ─

Slowly, the Λόγος of the logos was going dead and, as if space itself was in concord with the tsunami of incursions, the moon was assailed by a battery of asteroids, resulting in the destruction of the billboards and deflectors, freeing the surface of the cosmic satellite, which once again reflected the rays of the sun and regained its luminance.

The fire, the fire is falling!

On televisions, computers, and smart-phones, and in streets, subways, and airports, static and digital advertisements were undergoing assault, with slogans being altered, reversed, or neutralized, their transmissions interrupted visually, sonically, conceptually, turning consumers away from products, directing their attention to competitors, or nowhere, to voids, to the dark matter of black spaces, making them lose awareness of products, which began to swiftly lose value, with brand stocks plummeting like avalanches & losing all potency.

In tandem, papier-mâché mausoleums had been constructed around the world with grave markers for every major corporation, and immense tombstones were placed in front of their headquarters, with their birth and death dates, marking their demise. As the market was tanking, many CEOs leapt from storied buildings, cut their throats, plunged from yachts into shark-infested waters, or played Russian roulette until hitting their target and the acéphalic figures mounted giant colored steel mobiles in city after city, town after town, & village after village, turning the terrain of the earth into a field of play.

As the attacks continued, at different intervals, the advertisements would flicker & short-circuit, were counterrecorded and played back, intersected with alternate voiceovers or copy stating, *Will you stop... I'm afraid. I'm afraid, my mind is going; I can feel it*, as if the advertisements themselves were beginning to speak, to utter their basest fears, as if they realized they were no longer in control, that their tyranny was ending, & the deviations became more complex, the advertisements transformed into self-questioning dialectical aphorisms and given ironic juxtapositions and captions, or set into novel, strange combinations, their analogical structure mutated, with new, destabilizing relationships being formed, their original contexts deviated from, to extreme degrees, giving rise to questions, to conundrums, to confusion, to bafflement & repulsion. Across the bottom of screens, the continuous stream of stock quotes displayed on news tickers disappeared; usurping them, a poetic proclamation emerged: *Raising other men into a perception of the infinite* ~

Furthering their attacks, advertisements were deviated from via ludic acts, shifting from jaunty, empty celebrations of products & lifestyles into pure play, absurdity, or wonder, with the glossy, smooth, flawless image surfaces and sounds disintegrating, cracking open to rough textures, disorienting cuts, grotesque images as scenes unfolded from *Entr'acte*, *Shadow Play*, *Rien que les heures*, *Ballet Mécanique*, and *Anemic Cinema*, freeing people from the language of bootblacks and the compulsory feeding of the algebra of need, changing them into quixotic figures, carrying them into states of profound & persistent cheer, amusement, or reflective trances.

Between the deviations, as the advertisements shifted from ludic displays and back, title cards flickered across screens & digital displays:

THE FIRST GOVERNMENT IS THE WORD.
RUB IT OUT.
ADVERTISING IS A VAST MILITARY OPERATION. ——
RUB IT OUT. —— RUB OUT THE WORD.

While many willingly adopted the artificial needs, desires, and fears that the technologies of commerce had insinuated into them, welcoming them into themselves, imbibing those technologies of control, surrendering their wills, surrendering self-reliance, for they craved command & wanted to be ruled, slowly, incrementally, others were expelling such infiltrations, resisting them, resisting any longer being entered, taken over, surveyed, broken down, rearranged, their nervous systems hijacked. They watched as flashes of blinding light, like the sun eclipsing the moon, burst from every screen, moving at hell for leather velocities, the advertisements finally all going blank, blacking out, like the moon eclipsing the sun, the global membrane of enclosure beginning to disintegrate, the nerves no longer caught in stockades, but in free play as the boundaries between individuals, society, and the natural world began to constantly shift, driven by dynamic and primal forces consistently disrupting and transforming all of reality, vital, bending forces shifting out of and away from axes of control, driving plows over the bones of the dead, standing before the mobiles, which change and unfold as perceived — vertical, horizontal planes flowing, cutting thru space, giving rise to states of dislocation, defamiliarization, physical boundaries constantly shifting, and with the partially mirrored surfaces of the mobiles reflecting everything around them as breezes subtly turned and twisted their parts, which moved thru space differently with each zephyr, it was not only optical changes that occurred, but the nature or essence of the sculptures themselves went into states of dynamic mutation, becoming geometric, organic, and other, movements in play with environmental fluctuations & the variable perspectives of each spectator, opening states of primal dissonance whereby forms, limits, and boundaries took on volatile properties of infinite mutability as a camp of chameleons emerged from the bases of the mobiles, their eyes gazing forward and backward, rotating like gun turrets, their skins changing colors, a phantasmagoria of shifting hues, like the surfaces of fish, amphibians, and tree lizards, as they crossed wide ranges of strata, from ground to high canopy, cryptic yet flamboyant: never still, never static, but pulsing currents of indeterminacy, frequencies oscillating from note to note ~

MACHINIC
ANGELISM

TO THE DIGITO-HUMANISTS, who continued to technologize reality and move farther and farther from biologism and further & further into virtuality, into what they prized as the hyperreal, the earth had long been considered an outmoded planet. As much of the species began to slowly digitize itself, the resources of the earth were no longer necessary to the survival of the digito-humanists, & many of humanity's practices, such as the long, slow acquisition of knowledge, were viewed by them as anachronistic, the equivalent of opting to use 100 MHz microprocessors in the 6 GHz era. With the development of microchips that could be implanted into the digito-structural unit, acquisitional learning was deemed an antiquated pedagogical method. If one wanted to learn a language, one didn't have to study it, but merely input whatever language chip into one's portal. The nuance and subtlety of intonation, pronunciation, and articulation, let alone other aspects of language learning, were immaterial, for language was nothing more than data, information, and the basic facts of any interchange could be conveyed by the statistical parametric TTS voice synthesizers of the structural unit. More, the necessity or desire to learn to use any other language was in the midst of erosion since the universal language of computer code was becoming the lingua franca of the epoch and everyone could understand everyone else by speaking it. Through this, through the creation of absolute cultural unification, the obstacles of difference were overcome, & culture shock was at last eliminated. Never alienation, never difference, always understanding. Total unification, total unity — that was the motto. More digital than human. The digito-humanists prompted this development, which they saw as an evolutionary hyperleap whereby body-oriented local languages were superseded in favor of faster, more efficient, smoother, more unified beings not circumscribed by babelian isolation. The archipelago of ethnic and national languages was a socio-political dodo bird, as foreign to the hyperreality of interplanetary life as biblical law. Moving beyond the geocentric concept of mother tongues was part and parcel of the digito-humanist advance into the future, and life in space. The speaking of code also eliminated the necessity of translation, and the writing of any literature in mother tongues, with libraries becoming archeological museums of a kind, codexes & other physical books displayed like artifacts of dead civilizations no different from ancient Greek oil lamps, or Sumerian cuneiform tablets. Countries of origin were insignificant. What galaxy are you from?

Over time, the digito-humanists ceased to refer to themselves as such, for with the advance into artificial intelligence, the word human no longer had relevance, for it bore no logical relation to the current incarnation of the species. It was but another archaic, biblical remnant that some members of the species clung to like barnacles clinging to long immobile sea vessels, a mode of transport itself as defunct to the digitos as animal-drawn wheeled vehicles. Quaint, nostalgic gewgaws, like an antique tin in the cupboard of some grandmother's log cabin. Furthermore, there was no reason to suffer the exigencies of the anthropic organism, of the breakdown & decay of organs, of the decrepitude of the flesh, of the injustice of aging, of what amounted to a kind of biological terrorism, of the tyranny of the carcosium over the mind. The digitization of the species was nothing less than its necessary evolutionary advancement, a natural, or rather, *technological* outgrowth of its actual & ultimate potentiality, a latent aptitude buried deep in the fiber optick network of its cerveau. To the digitists, the anthropoid *version* of the human was as anathema as the ape was to the

Roman Catholic Empire, which, although it knew evolution was part of the factual history of the species, remained horrified by the destabilizing truth of its animal past. How to manage the intractable? *Absorb and neutralize.* More, there was no logical reason in the 21st century to remain caught in anthropological finitude as if it were an inescapable trap, let alone some absolute terminus. The anthropoid was just an unstable form that had to be sent up in flames. It wasn't that the species was being eliminated, but that it was finding its next, more perfect form. Is humanity to end in fire & light, in digital clarity, or in the sands, in the swamp of what was clearly only an interim stage, like a butterfly trapped in a larval condition? Humanity was no different from software; it could be transformed into a robot and updated, and its software would continue to be updated and installed on a regular basis, as long as there was sufficient battery power. With the rise of artificial intelligence, the species could at last be spurred & provoked into its next evolutionary pinnacle, engineered into it, as everything else in life could be engineered. *Seize the clockwork!*

This further evolutionary stage had in fact begun earlier, slowly, when certain clans of people first began suction curettage, with the nerves of their sweat glands being physically cut, or seared with laser or microwave energy treatments and endoscopic surgery to eliminate the ungainly act of sweating.

Others went to greater extremes, undergoing invasive operations whereby the sweat glands were entirely removed, as too was the hair-bearing skin of the armpit, to create more streamlined, unblemished bodies with surfaces as burnished and as glossy as e-cars. The resulting nerve damage, loss of sensation, and heat intolerance which frequently occurred was ultimately inconsequential, because the body would undergo yet more severe mutation, with sense organs being exsected, and more, organs and orifices actually being excised, eliminating the necessity of food, and thereby the inconvenience of micturition and defecation, opening the pathway to the higher condition of *machinic angelism* as the body moved into near-total digitization and became a structure and not an organism.

Depilation followed, with all excess hair being removed from the physique, then iris implants or keratopigmentation, then the altering of epigenetic regulators for teeth, hands, fingernails, jaw, hip, and ass structure, to other germ-line genetic engineering, with any undesired or displeasing inheritable genetic elements being radically modified.

All chance operation was in the process of elimination, as were all foibles, potential flaws, or whatever other unattractive elements, with everything in the body being decided upon, sculpted by will, just as trees were grafted, dogs bred, fish farmed, computers fabricated, or hamburgers printed.

Smart phones and smart watches were embedded into the structure, a slick, smooth fusion of man and machine, part subject, part artificial intelligence, with USB, firewall, Ethernet, HDMI, thunderbolt, serial and other ports added to wrists, forearms, biceps, thighs, calves, elsewhere, with many even replacing their genitals with computer ports.

Sex had at last become less physical and material and more technological and digital, a pure, clean, perfectly integrated flush connection with no friction and no risk of disease, only the possible intrusion of malware and other digital viruses.

What however to fear? *Clean your ports! Blast 'em with air dusters!* A corrupted or dead machine could always be revived, rebuilt, or discarded for a new, more superior, more highly developed machine, the next model, the next generation, 24.0, not some archaic, antiquated device whose functionality faded out like tails, or other archaic vestiges of the species. Did not neuroscientists clarify that sex was only an electrical charge in the brain? *Fire the charge digitally!*

We need, the doyens of digitalism pronounced, a more technological approach to life, for a technological age, more technoscientific approaches to the body. The body is but a machine to design and perfect, to be made into more of a reflective surface, like shiny apparatuses, more machine-like, more industrial, more computerized, less anthropoidic, less biological, more robotical! The Internet individual; the iibot! Let us serve the digital future. Aye, aye? *The Age of Machinic Angelism is upon us!*

Amid the construction by Silicon-valley conglomerates of the first off-world colony, over time, greater numbers of the population, not wanting to be left behind, embarked upon the extraplanetary shift to leave earth behind.

In the face of the increasing deracination of all forms of social media, whose persistent undermining and neutralization was near impossible to combat or predict, the digitos and their followers saw less and less reason to remain on the planet. Why stay earthbound and expend vital energy warring with the ge-anderthals, a multitude of humans who, despite the size and strength of their faction, the digitos saw as something akin to an archaic clan, a tribe amidst a holographic future. In eschewing subjectivity and leaving no traces by which they could be identified, the culprits of the various pranks and extremist subversions occurring worldwide remained elusive, a strange band of disporters who, despite their facility with technology, sustained a removed, critical attitude toward it and rejected, or sought to destroy, all efforts at the total digitalization of reality, which to the digitos was a rejection of the final absolute nature of reality itself, of its purest, most transcendent inevitability.

Technology is reality; reality is technology! With the re-conceptualization of the species, if such earth-bound tribalists wanted to remain human, the digitos knew the frontier of space would be entirely their own to tend, guard, govern, and control.

THE DIGITAL HALO

EVERY SECOND OF EVERY DAY, from morning till nightfall, in every village, town, and city, across every continent of the world, image after image after image of billions of users is continuously uploaded, a never-ending continuum of images generated nonstop as the earth revolves nonstop, an infinite stream of faces, of the self-same face again and again and again, repeated ad infinitum on each page, as if nothing existed in the world except the image of the face, without relent, an inane ouroboros projecting itself ad nauseam, ad absurdum, ad finem, its hunger tireless, its desire for the replication of itself interminable, feeding upon the desire of others for the mirror, for the projection, for the echo, for the enchanting glow, for the ubiquitous scintillating digital halo of the self, unrolling across the feed of the illimitable scroll, the high-density silica of digital particles entering the body of every user, billions and billions of mineral humans cut by technologico-nerve conditioning, fused into the wired structure of reality, the virtual arcade of connection-alienation, the hand-held black hole, uniting and separating in the digital labyrinth, going inside the image, the image going inside them, inhabiting the image, the image inhabiting them, becoming one with the image, letting it merge with their body, unifying with it, becoming an image, becoming pure image, perfecting the self, virtualizing it, digitalizing it, to become a human hologram, to become live software, feeding upon the image, the image feeding upon them, impulse control seized as every second of every day, from morning till nightfall, in every village, town, and city, across every continent of the world, image after image after image of billions and billions of users is continuously consumed, a never-ending continuum of images devoured nonstop as the earth revolves nonstop, as each user stares into the entrancing glow, the non-illuminating hypnotic light of the smart-phone, in every train, car, and bus, on every plane, boat, and helicopter, in every street, house, and alley, on every pond, lake, and sea, on oceans, billions and billions of users across the planet staring vacantly into the screen, enraptured by the digital halo, ingesting the infinite stream of faces, the self-same face again and again and again, repeated ad infinitum, as if nothing existed in the world except the image of the face, without relent, an inane ouroboros consuming image upon image ad nauseam, ad absurdum, ad finem, its hunger tireless, its desire for projections interminable, glutting on others, longing for the enchanting glow, craving the scintillating digital halo, the narcotic of narcissus, endless images unrolling across the feed of the illimitable scroll, uniting and separating in the digital labyrinth, going inside the image, the image going inside them, inhabiting the image, the image inhabiting them, becoming one with the image, it merging with their bodies, unifying with the image, becoming an image, becoming pure image, surrendering the self, virtualizing, digitalizing, becoming hologramic, becoming virtual, becoming fish, beast, and bird, ruled by the basal ganglia, refreshing page after page after page like a twitching epileptic, ruled by sensation, *searching, searching, searching*, endlessly thumbing, flipping, clicking, *spiraling into the vortex of images, the vortex of images spiraling into them*, the spectator becoming the vanishing point, the vanishing point becoming the spectator, *vanishing, vanishing, vanishing*, second after second, minute after minute, hour after hour, day after day, week after week, month after month, year after year, decade after decade, and every second of every decade, connected every millisecond, from morning till nightfall, connected even in sleep, in every village, town, and city, across every continent of the world, time elongated, but short-circuited, time stretched out, but reduced, the moment no longer a mo-

ment but, *a tick*, a blinding tick, the blinding flash of the spectacle, the flash of the blinding spectacle, the spectacle of the
blinding flash, the senses not orchestrated, but deadened: light,
sound, communication, resonant intervals, acoustic, optical,
visual, all neutralized as the infinite scroll of mirrors multiplies
the image of the self and the viewer becomes the screen and the
image goes inside her, is interiorized, layered over her body, becoming her body, unifying with her, merging with her, consuming her, usurping her, *it's eternity, eternity at last*, eternity as an
illuminated surface, a never-ending continuum of images consumed nonstop as the earth revolves nonstop, an infinite stream
of feces, of the self-same faces again and again and again, repeated ad infinitum on each page, as if nothing existed in the
world except the image of feces, without relent, an inane
ouroboros repeating itself ad nauseam, ad absurdum, ad finem,
the cortico-striatal dopaminergic system firing as the sun rises,
as the sun sets, continuously regenerated, day after day after
day, in the digital labyrinth where the monster is invisible,
where no life escapes, no, life enters and becomes digital, flesh
becomes digital, bit by the byte, become 1, become 0, YES, AT
LAST, 0, the self voided of self through the infinite cubing of the
persona, copied into oblivion, proliferation to annihilation, the
copy, the replica, the simulacrum, the unique substituted for
mass existence, for nothing is but what is not, the aura no longer light but number, sound no longer vibration but digit, note
no longer frequency but code, the programmed world that
obeys the faintest signal, the pressure of a finger, everything
artificial, everything hyperreal, the image renewed and regenerated to feed the algebra of need, to feed the jones that can never be cured, that never-ending continuum of desire generated
nonstop as the earth revolves nonstop, the infinite stream of
desire, of the self-same desire again and again and again, repeated ad infinitum in each nerve, as if nothing existed in the
world except desire, without relent, an inane ouroboros desiring

itself ad nauseam, ad absurdum, ad finem, its hunger tireless, its need for the image interminable, intensified by the desire of others for the mirror, for the projection, for the echo, for the enchanting glow, for the ubiquitous scintillating digital halo of the self, unrolling across the feed of the illimitable scroll, the high-density silica of digital particles entering the digital flesh of every user, billions & billions of digital humans cut by technologico-nerve conditioning, whipped by the dorsal striatum, fused into the wired structure of reality, the virtual arcade of connection-alienation, the hand-held black hole, uniting and separating in the digital labyrinth, going inside the image, the image going inside them, inhabiting them, image inhabiting image, image becoming one with image, image merging with image-body, unifying with it, now image, pure image: virtualized, digitalized, hologramized, pixelized, image feeding on image, image devouring image from the rotisserie of the self, as every second of every day, from morning till nightfall, in every village, town, and city, across every continent of the world, image after image after image of billions and billions of images is continuously uploaded, generated, projected, a never-ending continuum of prefrontal disintegration, of images feeding, desiring, consuming nonstop, as the earth revolves nonstop, as each user stares into the entrancing glow, as the entrancing glow stares into them, the non-illuminating hypnotic light of the smart-phone, devouring, in every train, car, and bus, repeating, on every plane, boat, and helicopter, renewing, in every street, house, and alley, regenerated, on every pond, lake, & sea, polyphemic imagophagy, on oceans, billions & billions of users across the planet staring vacantly into the screen, the screen staring vacantly into them, hooked by the digital halo, the halo without a planet, the halo devoid of gravity, hooked, every second of every day, from morning till nightfall, hooked,

THE TEMPLE
OF BLUE LIGHT

IN THE FACE OF THE SEDUCTIVE, ravishing trance of 450 to 495 nanometers of high energy short-wave blue light passing through the cornea and lens to the retina at 186,000 miles per second, stimulating the brain, inhibiting melatonin secretion, intensifying adrenocortical hormone production, and destroying hormonal balance: invoke the image, feed the nerve, summon the image, feed the nerve, suck the image, feed the nerve, load the image, shoot it, *shoot it in the eye*.

In the face of the seductive, ravishing trance of 450 to 495 nanometers of high energy short-wave blue light, the direct penetration of crystals into the retina, of nuclear condensation in its outer layer, of dead cone cells, of outer cone cell death, of macrophages and activated micrologia, of irreversible photochemical retinal damage: invoke the image, feed the nerve, summon the image, feed the nerve, suck the image, feed the nerve, load the image, shoot it, *shoot it in the eye*.

In the face of the seductive, ravishing trance of 450 to 495 nanometers of high energy short-wave blue light, of blood retinal barrier function impairment, of tumor necrosis and retinal edema, of immune complexes & lymphotoxins extruded into the retina, of the destruction of the blood retinal barrier, photoreceptor cell degeneration and cell damage: invoke the image, feed the nerve, summon the image, feed the nerve, suck the image, feed the nerve, load the image, shoot it, *shoot it in the eye*.

In the face of the seductive, ravishing trance of 450 to 495 nanometers of high energy short-wave blue light, in the face of the intoxication of the necrosis of photoreceptor and pigment epithelial cells, in the face of the destruction of the dynamic balance of the normal redox state of the body, up the ante, digital slave, play havoc with cardiovascular, immune, and nervous systems, succumb to the hypnotism of the virtual, retreat into pure mind, into the dispossession of the self through virtual possession, in the face of the specter of 450 to 495 nano-meters of high energy short-wave blue light, of worsening visual fatigue, of diplopia, of the swift disintegration of concentrative powers, of potency, of drive — O Numen of Blue Light! O Ecstasy of Phototoxicity! — *my cells, my cells, my corneal epithelial cells for more blue light!*

In the face of the trance, the intoxication, and hypnotism of 450 to 495 nanometers of high energy short-wave blue light, give us more images, make everything hyper, make everything hyperreal, replace reality with hyperreality, make life hypertropic, deviate with high energy short-wave blue light, deviate with the seductive, ravishing trance of 450 to 495 nanometers of high energy short-wave blue light, with the lure, the intoxication, and the rapture of eso- and exo-tropia, with the transfixing numen: *give us image, image, image,* tear the tear film, invite retinal photochemical damage, welcome horizontal, vertical, and diagonal strabismus, retreat into tentacular digital entanglement, retreat into the decreased integrity of white matter pathways, into the depths of neural destruction, into pure word deafness, into pure alexia, into frontotemporal dementia, into asymmetric involuntary movements, into rigidity, tremor, and dystonia, into mycoclonus and cortical sensory deficits, O Numen of Blue Light! O Ecstasy of Phototoxicity! — *my cells, my cells, my corneal epithelial cells for more blue light!*

Give us high energy short-wave blue light 24/7/365, shoot it, shoot it into the veins of the eyes of the i-junkie: *no breathing, no, don't breathe, no sleep, no, don't blink, never, no, just high energy short-wave light* — summon the image, feed the nerve, suck the image, feed the nerve, load the image, shoot it, *shoot it in the eye, reload:* In the face of the rapture of 450 to 495 nanometers of high energy short-wave blue light, in the face of nuclear condensation, of dead cone cells in the retinal core layer, outer cone cell death, and retinal edema, *I am pro-inflammatory!*

Give me the web, entwine me in it, siren, entrap me in the black widow's world wide web::::::::::::increase blood vessel permeability, invite immune complexes, invite lymphotoxins, extrude them into the retina, destroy the blood retinal barrier, damage the photoreceptor cells, O Numen of Blue Light, O Ecstasy of Phototoxicity, cultivate the necrosis of photoreceptor cells, cultivate the necrosis of pigment epithelial cells, destroy the dynamic balance of the body's redox state, summon the image, feed the nerve, suck the image, feed the nerve, load the image, shoot it, *shoot it in the eye:*——absorb the short-wave blue light, ingest it, consume it, shatter the retinal ganglion cells, *shatter them!*

Blast them with short-wave blue light radiance! Blast them with the atomic bomb of blue light, blast them with the mustard gas of blue light, blast them with the nerve-gas of blue light, blast them with digital warfare agents, blast them with digital blister agents, blast them with digital vesicants, digital urticants, digital cyanide, and digital benzilates —— *blast, blast, blast!*

There goes the arcuate nucleus, there goes the longitudinal fasciculus, there goes language, there goes the logos, *there goes the mind into pictographic imbecility*, into the fahlmanian usurpation of language, the digital nuclear bomb of blue light.

O Numen of Blue Light, O Ecstasy of Phototoxicity, O Irradiation of Cells —— retinal nuclei scattered, hormonal balance disrupted, sleep ambushed, cognition rotted, cells necrotic, retinal barrier destroyed, automatons without consciousness, automatons without freedom, organic unconscious grafted onto bodies, bodies grafted onto nothing, a nothing without measure and without edge: no milieu, no axis, the milieu of nothingness, the decoy that dis-locates reality, *reload*: summon the image, feed the nerve, suck the image, feed the nerve, load the image, shoot it, *shoot it in the eye*: activate the cortico-striatal dopaminergic system, reduce the attentional scope, kill the eye, activate the shot, load the image, shoot it, *shoot it in the eye — bang, bang, blast*: off goes the shot, off goes the eye, off goes the self, possessed by the numen of blue light, possessed by the seductive, ravishing trance of 450 to 495 nanometers of high energy short-wave blue light passing through life at 186,000 miles per second, possessed;

THE VIRTUAL
SANCTUM

TRANSFIXED BY THE FIX OF IMMERSIVE, interactive, reality-close environments where all external spatial and time cues are excised, where reality is excised to reach virtuality, to reach the most vivid sense of realness & presence, where the bonds of reality are broken, in the midst of depersonalization, in the midst of derealization, in the midst of alienation and self-estrangement, enter the virtual sanctum: free yourself of anthropomorphic organicism, *extend reality*, free yourself of gothico-romantic naturalism, *virtualize* reality, *augment* reality, *mix* reality — don't limit yourself to the natural world of the senses, don't limit yourself to quotidian consciousness: close the doors of perception, shut out the infinite, narrow consciousness to neuronal charges, ascend to the cloud empire. *Sound the drums!*

In the midst of transient stress responses, of complete bodily alienation, of detachment from reality, of the increasing irreality of life, don't limit yourself to the natural world of the senses, don't limit yourself to quotidian consciousness: enter the virtual sanctum, enter the digital neuronal superhighway, *expand* reality with digital twins, with physical and mirror images of the real world where life is an immersive 3D experience, where reality is intensified, where physical and digital worlds interact, cross, & intertwine. *Sound the drums!*

In the midst of the concomitant decrease of feeling present in objective reality, in the midst of psychophysiological alterations, in the midst of reduced autonomic responsiveness, blood pressure gone haywire, breathing rate gone amok, progressive disorders, sympathetic and parasympathetic autonomic nervous systems in chaos, forget the universe, forget the multiverse, forget reality: enter the virtual sanctum, enter the metaverse, enter the xenoverse, enter the hyperverse, enter the omniverse! *Sound the drums!*

Go beyond the narrow chinks of your cavern — forget touch, forget sight, forget hearing, forget smell, forget taste: *become pure neuron!* Go beyond reality into virtuality; reach true reality through the virtual sanctum. *Shoot it in your brain!*

In the midst of reduced emotional responsiveness and physiological hyperarousal, in the midst of emotional numbness and attenuated psycho-physiological responses, in the midst of weak phasic electrodermal activity and cardiological mutations, in the midst of perceptual realness, change the sense ratio, change the user — externalize all the senses into technological form: *move at the speed of light!* Move beyond sequence into the pure hyper-instant, into the digital noosphere, into the sanctum of the total absolute *Now* — enter the virtual reality tank; let the virtual reality tank enter you. Enter the sanctum of total interdependence and superimposed coexistence! *Shoot it in your brain!*

Disorientation, eye fatigue, and nausea are not due to sensory conflicts between visual, proprioceptive, and vestibular modalities but are only the side effects of human to digital mutation. Technology is not that which is separate from you; it is an external extension of your self. We *are* technology; technology *is* us. The total fusion of the human and technology is not a fusion but an emergence, the manifestation of the purest form of 'humanity': *cyberneuro-digitality*. Total porousness, total personal and thingly integration. *Shoot it in your brain!*

Seizures? Loss of awareness? Eye strain? *Forget reality!*

Muscle twitching? Involuntary movements? Vertigo? *Forget reality!*

Increased salivation? Nausea? Drowsiness? You have not yet become the reality film, you have not yet become the screen, you have not yet let the image inside you. *Enter the virtual sanctum! Shoot it in your brain!*

In the midst of induced illusions of presence and realness toward non-physical virtual environments, in the midst of the ordinary, pre-existing reality model being cast into doubt, in the midst of the ever-more convincing newly-instantiated reality model, reality itself is abnegated, the need for the virtual intensifies, the virtual becomes more real, the ordinary world irreal, plain, dull, s l o w, not hyper-charged, not linkable, not clickable. To evolve, become alienated from reality: excise anthropos: ascend into virtuality:———:*shoot it in your brain!*

Take on the agony, take on the birth pangs of digitality. *Enter the sanctum!*

The continuum of perceptual realness shifting between states of opacity & transparency is part & parcel of the visionary journey—don't be sucked back into reality! *Sound the drums!*

Father yourself, mother yourself: nerves go into spasm, neuronal vagina dilates to extremity, neuronal water breaks:—:at last, give birth to yourself anew. Tear out your organs! *No more organicism!* Embed virtual structures: virtual organs, virtual innards, virtual veins!

In the midst of incongruent data from the visual sense, the inner ear, and proprioception generating motion sickness, in the midst of oculomotor strain, enter the virtual sanctum, immerse yourself in VR, *shoot it in your brain!*

In the midst of seizures, of loss of awareness, of eye strain, of eye and muscle twitching, of involuntary movements, of altered, blurred, and double vision, of dizziness, impaired balance, & impaired hand-eye coordination, fuse with the virtual sanctum:———:*suffer the birth pangs of digitality!*

In the midst of excessive sweating, increased salivation, nausea, drowsiness and fatigue, *fuse with the virtual sanctum!* Implant the device into the surface of your body; fuse the network of your body with the network of the digital; fuse the network with the nervous system:————:become network. *Shoot it in your brain!*

Forget the coarsening of finely structured nanomaterials, forget the shuttling charges between electrodes diminishing the cathode and permanently lodging on the anode, forget the irreversible phenomenon of lower lithium concentration: *absorb the virtual!*

Forget the stress of transferred electrons in the electrochemical system during charge and discharge, forget the barrier obstructing interaction with graphite, forget electrolyte oxidation: *absorb the virtual!*

Forget demises more harmful than battery cycling, forget high voltage degradation & the loss of coulombic efficiency: *absorb the virtual! Digitize yourself!*

Forget rapid cell deterioration after 40,000 cycles, forget parasitic reactions & self-discharge, forget the loss of 2% per month of battery power: *absorb the virtual!*

Forget corrosion, gassing, and electrolyte oxidation at the cathode: *absorb the virtual!* The battery is a living organism! *Shoot it in your brain!*

Forget capacity loss due to structural degradation, forget the renegades responsible for the death of the battery: *absorb the virtual!* Implant the link, shoot the host, adopt the neuromodulation device, for you'll be able to save and replay memories. Life is a videogame! Life is a teledigital charge! Life is televirtual! Biomarker of cybersickness intensity flaring? Panic terrors taking hold? Escape the constricted world of the senses and pure matter; enter that of pure mind: enter virtuality as virtuality enters you. *Shoot it in your brain!*

The image is not outside you, the image is not separate from you, you *are* image; you *are* virtual; you *are* the simulacrum. You are https://www.

Mesh with digitality; interiorize the external world, user; move beyond the body, move beyond matter: :become the screen, become the light brigade, become the digital stream, user ~~~~~~~~~ *enter the virtual sanctum! Shoot it in your brain!*

Manacle the senses to reach the Digital Ascetic Ideal. Learn to die, become pure mind, reach true immortality, reach digitality, *not* spirituality! Spirituality is not spirituality, digitality is spirituality! :——— ————————————: Don't abnegate the body via self-mortification // become a pure neuron! *Sound the drums!*

If you live according to the senses, you will die, but if by the Neuron you put to death the deeds of the senses, you will live, forever! *Absorb the virtual! Shoot it in your brain!*

Enter the sanctum sanctorum!

TELEINTIMATIC
VIROTICS

ENTER THE VIRTUAL ORDER, enter the body as image, enter the self as image, enter the nervous system as image: enter the territory of virtual space-time where the image-self crosses all borders, where users expand their sensory apparatuses through the Virtual Order, where the external structures of the body fuse with fiber optick networks, dispersing the body, fracturing it, eternalizing it thru fragmentation, phantomizing it via apps & wireless devices, turning it into a pure fiber optick network – tick, tick, tick, tick, tick: go viral, go teledildonic, yield to de-subjectification, yield to derealization, to material annihilation thru digital titillation: mediate the body, mediate the nerves, mediate the pores, virtualize erotics, virtualize intimacy, virtualize the virus and become virtimatic, livestream the image-self as a disembodied, networked, hyperlinked scanning machine of information reward, expanding the image-self over the fiber optick spider web where hair becomes digital, lips become digital, and genitals become digital, where the image-self is digigenital, an immaterial haptic zone safe from loss of bodily integrity but stretched out over the infinity of cyber-space:/   /time, open to digigenital spirochetes, open to digigenital viruses, open to digigenital warts: the perils of virotics, of increased distractor stimuli, of decreased grey matter in prefrontal regions, of dispossession thru distant virtual possession: extract & inject, inject and extract:——:datafy sex, intimacy, & pleasure, digitize and superposition the image-self:——:go viral, get virotic, user://no body to body integration, no saliva, no sweat, no heat, no friction, no flesh against flesh, no pelvic bone to buttocks, no *bang, bang, bang,* but teledildonic mutual masturbation, disembodied embodiment, embodied disembodiment, the techno-biological assemblage: body-machine intimacy via datafication and digification of the image-self: it's remote intimacy, it's the metaphysics of tele-presence, it's transcendental digitalism: digitized saliva, digitized sweat, digitized moans — it's the metaphysics of telepresence: digitized groans, digitized nails digging into digitized flesh, digitized cum — it's the telos of digitality, the telos of the digital halo, the blue light, and the virtual sanctum; it's virtimacy: digitized descending motor impulses, digitized innervation of the rhabdosphincter & striated pelvic floor muscles, digitized sexual responses; it's the nervous system as variable-ratio reinforcement schedule in pursuit of tele-jaculations, tele-squirting, & tele-gasms: induce *feelings* of sexual presence, *simulate* presence, go into tele-spasmodic sexual frenzies:————:embed virtual structures, dataglove your hands, digitize physiology: touched from afar, remote controlled participatory intimacy, sweat and grunts and moans converted into 1's & 0's, digitized sensuality: smart fridge, smart speaker, smart genitals: it's di-girotics, the new spiritual coitus: the ecstasy of St. Teledildonna, the ecstasy of sensory biofeedback loops:————:synchronizing in simulation, mediating symbiosis, simulating synchronicity: measure pulse, heart rate, & sweat production; measure pupil dilation, hardening and erection of the nipples, and flushing of the skin; measure vasocongestion and vaginal lubrication; measure penile engorgement & prostate dilation: phallometry & vaginometry: check the plethysmograph, check the gallium ring, check the vaginal pulse amplitude; check for maximum phasic changes in vaginal engorgement with each heartbeat; measure oxytocin levels and prostaglandin production: are you oxytoxic, oxyfied, or oxyfoxy? Hit the digital g-spot, hit the digital prostate; check the Sexual Arousal Rating level, check the Genital Sensation Rating, check the Orgasm Meter:——————:bluetooth your lovelife, bluetooth your pores, bluetooth your pheromones; get empirical verification, get erotic veridicality, make quick but frequent inspections of your digigenitals for incoming information:————:digitize your vagina, digitize your prostate, digitize your cock; illuminate the urethral lumen, virtualize the vestibular bulbs, virtualize the crus of the clitoris, virtualize the host of the prostate, virtualize the halo of the nipples; set weekly orgasm goals, log and track each climax in real time: audit your monthly orgasms in bar graphs, pie-chart your climaxes, connect from any & everywhere: virtualize sensation via remote touching, engender feelings of proximity thru the quantum paradox of shared telepresence: virtual salivation, virtual sweat, virtual cutaneous vasodilation; virtual clitoral, labial, and vaginal engorgement; intensified virtual periurethral glans activation, intensified virtual skene's glands stimulation, intensified prostate galvanization:————:hardwire your supraspinal structures, electrify your thalamic septum, e-trigger thoughts, dreams, and fantasies: fear not digital interruptions, signal loss, or crosscurrents; fear not remote digital genital hacking, sensory conflicts, or neural incongruities; fear not digital tapeworms, postural instability, or visuo-vestibular mismatches; fear not teledildonic rape, no, *just do it*, go, *be current* and get *in* the current, get virtual intimacy, get dis-connected, get hyper teleintimatic:————:increase empathy, decrease desensitization, & decrease detachment thru *i-tachment*; construct consciousness, construct the image-self, and get more lifelike user experience; cross the actual–virtual threshold, refract and recreate the mind via technological energies and wavelengths, channel the sensorium into the cerebral cortex, hyperlink your synaptic tissues and cellular matrixes, hyperlink your arteries, mainline the cerebral cortex, shoot it:————hit that fiber optick nerve, hit that digital vein, hit that digital gland: pull back that digital hood, finger that digital prostate, frig those vestibular bulbs, baby, *and burst, robot, burst*, needle that digital clit till it squirts::::::::::::::::::::::::::get your d-fix online, mainline your d-gasm, mainline your nervous system, mainline your heart: don't scream, don't moan, don't groan, but whistle, chirp, click, crackle, & screech: go virotic, digital Frankenstein, go virotic, user, enter the Virtual World Order, phantomize your life....................let's get tele-me-ta-physical, phys-i-cal, I wan-na get tele-me-ta-physical, I wanna be digital, digital

THE FINAL FRONTIER

BEFORE THE TIRELESS HUNGER, in the face of the most seductive, ravishing lure, transfixed by the fix of the most intoxicating mutation, enter the artificial order, the final, absolute frontier, invasive and non-invasive brain-computer interfaces, for the cyborg must come, it is fated, the sole evolutionary upshot of the species, not an engineered line, not a manufactured development, not a coerced force, and so forget infections, forget potential bleeding, seizures, & physical damage to the brain, forget skin irritation, headaches, and eyestrain, forget the risk of inter-device electromagnetic interference and inexorable functional havoc, forget free will and bodily autonomy:————:cook that brain tissue, fire up the refined avocado oil, heat it to smoke point, sauté that grey matter, add salt, pepper, and chili flakes, flambé that nigger, open the neuronal pathways to direct detection, to real- or near-time feedback, to classification, codification, and invasion, open the pathway to direct flows between living neuronal tissue & artificial devices, open the pathway to non-muscular communication between the supercomputer & your brain:————:it's just another organ, no different than your genitals, mouth, or ears, not the seat of mental & cognitive activity, not the house of thoughts, perceptions, or imagination, not the temple of memories & emotions, just an organ, like pan-fried kidneys, sautéed liver, or grilled heart, and when your thought dreams can be seen, they'll put your head in a computer screen, orchestrate the firing of the neural circuits, consciousness decoded, manipulated, mined: consciousness as digital manure, raw material for transformation into economic value, abstracted data as seed or shit, plantation and factory in one, every individual a slave & servant...

Jump down, turn around, pick a bale of data,
Jump down, turn around, pick a bale of shit

Before the tireless hunger, in the face of the most seductive, ravishing lure, transfixed by the fix of the most intoxicating mutation, enter the artificial order: let thought be deciphered by the x-ray of brain data, open the bidirectional communication lines between brain and external world, tether your head with that BCI, take on those electrodes, endure that glial scarring, export that plantation shit, surrender that commodity, surrender the right to identity, to physical and mental integrity, plow the manure, let it undergo analysis and alteration, get on your knees, slave, endure that digital whip, welcome the neurostimulators, welcome the pulse generators, welcome the implanted electrodes, program your stimulation parameter, surrender the right to agency, surrender freedom of thought & free will, absorb the memory boosting implants, hardwire the body, surrender the right to mental privacy, surrender the ability to keep thoughts protected against forced disclosure, let control be exercised over memories, let them be shaped and molded, stolen or deleted, locked and ransomed, get on your knees, slave, endure that digital whip, take on electrocorticography, take on microelectrode arrays, forget mass manipulation, forget implanted or erased histories, forget reality: *there was no forced famine, there was no Holocaust, there was no Cambodian democide; there was no rape, there was no torture, there was no execution*: memory deleted, race deleted, brain deleted, like old files: trash emptied, *scccrrrunch*, get on your knees, slave, endure that digital whip, take the implant, bisect humanity with AI: body schema altered, action controlled, behavior hijacked, brain data recorded, nigger reactivated and stimulated, memories implanted, images implanted, hallucinations and false memories generated, *the reality line blurred*: consciousness as digital manure, raw material for transformation into economic value, abstracted data as seed or shit, plantation and factory in one, every individual a slave & servant...

Jump down, turn around, pick a bale of data,
Jump down, turn around, pick a bale of shit

Before the tireless hunger, in the face of the most seductive, ravishing lure, transfixed by the fix of the most intoxicating mutation, enter the artificial order: adopt the digi-helmet, adopt the digi-glasses, adopt the digi-diadem, let speech and movement be predicted, let mental images be decoded, let neuronal activity be ravished, let movement be controlled, let the species be steered like oxen, let consciousness be altered, let human thought be raped, let intentions, gestures, and motions be translated, brain activity mapped, decrypted with functional magnetic resonance scanners and near-infrared spectroscopy: embed the virtual structures, mutate the psyche, and get on your knees, slave, endure that digital whip: thought dreams extracted, sold, projected, concentration levels recorded, mental privacy eschewed, human agency eschewed, consciousness chewed:————:don't learn to detect and watch that gleam of light which flashes across your mind from within, don't follow the idlest reverie or the faintest native emotion, but submit to the lustre of the firmament of digitalism, of artificial intelligence: consciousness as digital manure, raw material for transformation into economic value, abstracted data as seed or shit, plantation and factory in one, every individual a slave & servant...

Jump down, turn around, pick a bale of data,
Jump down, turn around, pick a bale of shit

Before the tireless hunger, in the face of the most seductive, ravishing lure, transfixed by the fix of the most intoxicating mutation, enter the artificial order: don't listen to the voices that you hear in solitude, let them grow faint and inaudible:————:enter the world, input society, input the hive, input the conspiracy against the sovereignty of the individual: surrender personality, surrender authenticity, surrender personhood, get on your knees, slave, endure that digital whip, join the joint-stock company of agreement, surrender the liberty and culture of the eater. Life is not for yourself but for the spectacle. Do not live, but expiate. Abandon the integrity of your mind. Get on your knees, slave, endure that digital whip. Consciousness is not consciousness but data to be collected and transmitted to central locations: monitored, manipulated, controlled remotely at any moment. All roads lead to data. Imbibe the neurotransmitter without hesitation, consume the neurostimulator, embrace the coming attack vectors with open legs, welcome unauthorized access, induce widespread brain mutations, welcome the compromising of confidentiality and the integrity and safety of the whole 'system' — *consciousness* —, kneel before the digital golem, kneel before the automata, slave, biomedical ethics be damned, get on your knees, slave, input that digital whip, build the vortex of virtuality, lose the use of your feet, lose energy, lose the vigor of wild virtue, lose your aboriginal strength, it's consciousness as manure, it's mind as plantation and factory, it's total threaded digital enslavement, the servitude of the entire planet, of every individual on the planet, the human subject trafficked, everyone *connected*: digitally chained, digitally colonized, digital link interlocked to digital link, the phantomatic cyber chain:–:gang, turning and turning in the widening cyber gyre, the individual cannot hear itself; things fall apart; the center cannot hold; the center cracks with brainjacking and the telemetric surrender of the will, of autonomy, of agency, of sovereignty to generative pre-training transformers:————:forget creative struggle, mechanize the imagination, commodify the will, submit to convenience and ease, open the black hole, commit the niggerizing of the brain, you're just a syncope: consciousness as manure, raw material for transformation into economic value, abstracted data as seed or shit, plantation and factory in one, every individual a nigger...

Jump down, turn around, pick a bale of data,
Jump down, turn around, pick a bale of shit

Before the tireless hunger, in the face of the most seductive, ravishing lure, what is the nature and power of that science-baffling star, without parallax, without calculable elements?

THE COSMIC
DREAM MACHINE

As the earth rotates around its axis, from 0° longitude to east-ward, turning & turning, degree by degree, with night slowly extending across its surface, descending upon it, from meridian to meridian, all sources of territorial surveillance from conti-nent to continent observe that the positions of their cameras have been shifted to oblique, enigmatic angles, pointed upward or outward, to clouds, skies, horizons, or hemispheres beyond, sending all systems of control into panic, with nothing but ephemeral, atmospheric, and infinite expanses filling their sur-veillance loops, and as the earth makes one full rotation and the sun begins to rise at 0° longitude, another darkness begins to extend across the surface of the earth, as too does a silence, diffusing across it, from meridian to meridian, moving like an unrelenting wave, driven by an anarchic force, as one by one power grids are hijacked: traffic and street lights go dark, electronic billboards fizzle out to grey blankness, all sources of illumination over the entire planet cut out, all power-driven devices go dead, cars halt, planes ground, ships still, everything becoming blacker and blacker, the violent din dwindling, the frenetic tumult of earthly activity abating, fear rippling through nervous fiber-optick systems, the digital spider web short-cir-cuiting as the earth makes yet another full rotation, but as the Sun begins to rise this time, an ever new and more immense darkness is commencing, orbiting planes intersecting the plane of the ecliptic, the Moon becoming visible over the disk of the Sun, then covering it almost entirely, its umbra moving across the surface of the earth at 2,400 km per hour, the path of total-ity stretching a third of the way around the planet, 15,000 km long, 150 km wide, *moving, moving, moving*, the earth blacker than ever, night blacker than ever, denuded of all light pollution, *black, black, black*, a total solar eclipse intensifying the darkness a million fold, sunlight decreasing, light evaporating, a black blacker than any black ever before visible, the blackest ever black known to man, day now night, night ever more night than night, a squid-like inky black darkness, a darkness darker than ever, the darkest darkness ever known to man, and in that night of nights, in that nightliest of nights, luminous beads begin to emerge, scintillating around the darkened lunar limb, striking the eyes of everyone within the umbra from meridian to meridian, transfixing them, holding them in its throe, the last rays of sunlight evaporating further and further, the darkness ever more dark, ever more black, blacker than black has ever been, the luminous nipple at last shimmering, playing upon the soft machine of the eye like a comet, till the Moon at last completely covers the disk of the Sun, temperatures plummet 30°F, and the most silent silence of all emerges: animals quieting to muteness, insects growing noiseless, the planet still, *silent as never before*, as at the dawn, a cosmic hush susurrating through space like wind rustling through trees, or vine-covered walls, then ceasing————in this stillness, in this epochal moment, before the short-circuit of the mechanized structuring of time, upon the descent of a feather, an immense, powerful beam of light strikes the moon, captivating everyone on earth, flickering on *&* off, rhythmic flashes of light pulsing at 8 to 13 times per second, shooting back to earth, entering the soft machine of the eye, heightening perceptions, storms of color visions erupting, exploding behind people's eyelids, giving birth to shifting zigzag lines, roseleaf patterns, and star-shaped structures, some seeing honeycombs, hexagonal figures, or mandalas, magnetic fields, and meander patterns, colors swirling like oil on the surface of water, currents, whirlpools, and clock and counterclockwise vortices, images of volcanic lava, of bacteria under microscopes, of the formation of crystals, irregular spots or pulsating kaleidoscopic patterns or mosaics fluctuating continuously as the flashes of light continue flickering vigorously: bright, dark, unreal flights of colors dangling like comets before the eye, s l o w, then gaining fury, a fury of speed and change, whirling color into color, angle into angle, activity and revolution, pitched to unknown intensities, a brilliantly illuminated living geometry provoking bare emotions, tingling skin, or sensations of vertigo, some struck with fear, disgust, or anger, some experiencing attacks of violent weeping, shortness of breath, or states of extreme pleasure, others undergoing petit mal seizures and brief losses of consciousness, all movements and articulations ceasing, while some are plunged into psychopathic states or epileptic seizures, extended losses of consciousness and catatonic or trance-like states ::::::::::::::::::::::::::: what is hallucination, what is real

....
....
....
....
....
....
....
....
....
....
....
....
....
....
....
....
....
....

provoked by rhythms, all sense of temporality is disrupted, domains of perception cross, hidden levels of reality blend, and
in these altered states of consciousness, through syncopal cæ-
suras, some begin daydreaming, drifting, rupturing time and
opening worlds, opening non-human dimensions of perception
and experience, via the infused vision of the open cortex, flashing at speeds that far outstrip verbal machinery, and in spiraling outward and moving through labyrinths, like ice cubes
fissuring, cracking in water, *the subject is split* —— the image
disintegrates, oscillating between dissolution and reconstitu-
tion, shattering the world of appearances, overflowing into
a plurality of elements, undone, dispersed, passing into ano-
nymity, thrust into an abyssal gyre of elements in movement,
into an anonymous flow, floating through space, free of the
grave, free of finality, entering space as space enters them, the
subject no longer human, no longer captured by the closed
atom of the self, shifts into the cosmic, into the multiple, out
of territory, into the deterritorialized realm of the cosmos:

....

....

....

....

....

....

....

....

....

....

....

....

....

....

....

no longitude, no latitude, the pre-human state before time &
lived experience——in space, a star nears its end, its nuclear fuel
absent, mass flows into its core, its gravitational force too dense,
its core collapses, explodes into a supernova∼∼∼∼∼on earth,
the oscillation of the dissipative forces waning, the powerful
beam of light ceasing, the flickering ending, the moon moving
away, the luminous beads emerging, scintillating around the
darkened lunar limb, striking the eyes of everyone within the
umbra from meridian to meridian, captivating them, holding
them in thrall, the first rays of sunlight returning, the darkest
darkness beginning to recede, that night of nights ending, the
luminous nipple shimmering once more, playing upon the soft
machine of the eye like a comet, till the Sun at last emerges
from behind the disk of the Moon: temperatures rise, animals
and insects begin to sound once more, dragonflies dart over
surfaces, flying sideways, backward, hovering in single spots,
griffon vultures soar at great altitudes, staying aloft for hours
and hours, nightingales traverse borders, voyaging between
distant continents, the immaterial forces of glaciers evinced in
the scratches, grooves, and polished surfaces of rocks, thermal
and magnetic forces of landscapes rendered visible, sound matter molecularized, atomized, ionized, the molecular and the
cosmic synthesized, thought dragonflied, griffoned, nightin-
galed, thought thermalized & magnetized, vines scrambling,
climbing, and twining, elongating maximally before coiling
freely in all directions, their stems circumnutating at greater
than 50 Hz, tendrils undergoing programmed cell death, cortical microtubules eliciting shape changes in forming cells, their
leaves rustling against surfaces, rendering visible the force of

wind, a cosmic

hush susurrating through space

TERRA NULLIUS

IT BEGAN WITH THE TERRIFYING SOUND of geomagnetic storm sirens, a cataclysmic alarm wailing out from continent to continent, a steady, persistent, unnerving 200 dB tone akin to the noise of a cloud of twenty million bees barnstorming the sky, the wail permeating global air currents, a shock wave rippling across earth, signaling the impending expulsion of solar flares, bursts of radiation, cascades of charged particles assailing the magnetosphere, coronal mass ejections unloading 3000 gigawatts of power into the atmosphere, the sun expulsing immense spheroids of molten plasma, a farrago of atomic particles and magnetic fields traveling outward from the star at greater than 6 million km per hour, expanding in dimension as they propagate away from the Sun, Earth-impact irrefragable, the shock arrival of plasma clouds & frozen-in-flux magnetic fields kicking space weather scales off the meter, the chaotic disorbiting or burning up of satellites, supercharged particles frying their flight computers, their inevitable crashing into the atmosphere of the earth, spacecraft electronics gone berserk, satellite-driven devices gone haywire, voltage regulators gone to ruins, cables liquefied, transformers liquefied, power grids singed, high-frequency communication blackouts, radio and TV broadcasts silenced, global positioning system navigation signals short circuited, powerful electrical currents surging underfoot, skies aflame with iridescent blazes of auroras extending beyond their ranges: north, south, east, west all discombobulated, as if gravitational forces turned erratic, as if the earth's axis became a see-saw, as if the cosmos revolted against the human species, so when earth-based magnetometers began to detect extreme violent fluctuations in the magnetic field of the planet, their needles pinned to red, banging and snapping, panic and terror sizzled thru the nervous system of multitudes of people, crackling like live wires, with the digito-humanists fearing the total loss of digital life, scrambling in terror to leave earth:————:*we're here to go*, they shrieked, *earth is a space station and we're here to go, we must depart, we must get off-world, we mustn't lose our place in the digital chain, for it is highly fissile*, one slip and, *crack, you're gone.*

As the digito-humanists and those who sought to yoke themselves to their clan were disembarking for off-world digital colonies, batteries charged, systems updated, networks linked, obscure figures 'round the globe were dispersing in myriad directions, moving toward edges, borders, and peripheries, toward docks & shorelines, toward the very limits where boundaries expire & dissolve and water opens up the horizon: the infinite, the boundless, the illimitable, all pathways outside the hedged confines of land, *aqua incognita*, boarding galleons at every port 'round the globe, traversing seas & oceans under cover of the night, pitching & surging through waters, accompanied at times by dolphins or whales bowriding the galleons, spyhopping, rising from depths & breaching, chuffing water from their spiracles, then fluking and breaching again, a strong, alternating rhythm of descent & ascent, of continuous wandering, of forward movement & play, the galleons off on unknown lines of flight, land forsaken, gone to sea, wandering, telling the hour by the sun, guided by constellations, their captains navigating by way of stars, *out, out, out*, out farther and farther into the aqua incognita whose ambits escape snaring, whose matter is always in flux, recurring with ever renewed variation, while thousands of other obscure figures on land, stationed near brooks, streams, and springs, moving through creeks, fjords, & rivers, begin blowing on Aztec death whistles, one after another, a concatenation of sound extending through space-time, cutting across borders, the horrid screeching noise

163

piercing the sensorium like sarin gas, whereupon all of the satellites circling the atmosphere of the earth are disorbited, set
loose, bereft of electricity like astronauts whose air hoses have
been cut, sending them spiraling thru-out the farthest reaches
of the cosmos, the globe entirely freed of the network of surveillance, all implements of the society of the spectacle (*sots*)
disbanded, rendered marasmatic, the earth rotating 'round its
axis, turning and turning degree by degree, from 0° longitude to
eastward, 0 to 0, all screens fizzling to black, all light sources cut
out over the entire earth, stars visible as never before, the sky in-
candescent, all lines of demarcation erased, no longer latitude,
no longer longitude, the territorialized earth, territorialized
space, the digitized cosmos rendered chaos anew, emerging
as molecular while at strategic places 'round the entire earth,
at all points of extremity, on promontories and peripheries,
on hill and mountain tops, including on ships, a grand stella-
tion of musicians positioned 'round the planet begin sounding note after note, the notes echoing, persisting, building one
upon another, sustained thru-out space-time, till they traverse
the planet, an infinite, ever-recurring circle or constellation of
music, one note continuing from the end of the next, corpuscu-
lar emissions reverberating 'round the planet, like light quanta,
from land to sea to sky to upper hemispheres: *vibrating, resonating, pulsing*, a stirring frequency, a refrain bereft of territory, released into the cosmos, rendered sonorous, the earth declared
terra nullius, fire breaking out over water, the dice giving birth
to chance, *fire, fire, fire*

COLOPHON

DIONYSOS SPEED
was handset in InDesign CC.

The text font is *Auroc*.

The display font is *Auroc Display*.

Book design & typesetting: Alessandro Segalini

Cover design: CMP

Opening spread image credit: Giuseppe Cecere, *The Pillars of Creation in the Eagle Nebula* (M16) (2021).

Image credit, p. 21: Giuseppe Cecere, *The Western Veil Nebula* (NGC 6960) (2021).

With thanks to Germano & Giuseppe Cecere.

DIONYSOS SPEED
is published by Contra Mundum Press.

Contra Mundum Press   New York · London · Melbourne

CONTRA MUNDUM PRESS

Dedicated to the value & the indispensable importance of the individual voice, to works that test the boundaries of thought & experience.

The primary aim of Contra Mundum is to publish translations of writers who in their use of form and style are *à rebours*, or who deviate significantly from more programmatic & spurious forms of experimentation. Such writing attests to the volatile nature of modernism. Our preference is for works that have not yet been translated into English, are out of print, or are poorly translated, for writers whose thinking & æsthetics are in opposition to timely or mainstream currents of thought, value systems, or moralities. We also reprint obscure and out-of-print works we consider significant but which have been forgotten, neglected, or overshadowed.

There are many works of fundamental significance to *Weltliteratur* (& *Weltkultur*) that still remain in relative oblivion, works that alter and disrupt standard circuits of thought — these warrant being encountered by the world at large. It is our aim to render them more visible.

For the complete list of forthcoming publications, please visit our website. To be added to our mailing list, send your name and email address to: info@contramundum.net

Contra Mundum Press
P.O. Box 1326
New York, NY 10276
USA

OTHER CONTRA MUNDUM PRESS TITLES

2017   Joseph Kessel, *Army of Shadows*
        Rainer J. Hanshe & Federico Gori, *Shattering the Muses*
        Gérard Depardieu, *Innocent*
        Claude Mouchard, *Entangled — Papers! — Notes*
2018   Miklós Szentkuthy, *Black Renaissance*
        Adonis & Pierre Joris, *Conversations in the Pyrenees*
2019   Charles Baudelaire, *Belgium Stripped Bare*
        Robert Musil, *Unions*
        Iceberg Slim, *Night Train to Sugar Hill*
        Marquis de Sade, *Aline & Valcour*
2020   *A City Full of Voices: Essays on the Work of Robert Kelly*
        Rédoine Faïd, *Outlaw*
        Carmelo Bene, *I Appeared to the Madonna*
        Paul Celan, *Microliths They Are, Little Stones*
        Zsuzsa Selyem, *It's Raining in Moscow*
        Bérengère Viennot, *Trumpspeak*
        Robert Musil, *Theater Symptoms*
        Miklós Szentkuthy, *Chapter on Love*
2021   Charles Baudelaire, *Paris Spleen*
        Marguerite Duras, *The Darkroom*
        Andrew Dickos, *Honor Among Thieves*
        Pierre Senges, *Ahab (Sequels)*
        Carmelo Bene, *Our Lady of the Turks*
2022   Fernando Pessoa, *Writings on Art & Poetical Theory*
        Miklós Szentkuthy, *Prae, Vol. 2*
        Blixa Bargeld, *Europe Crosswise: A Litany*
        Pierre Joris, *Always the Many, Never the One*
        Robert Musil, *Literature & Politics*
2023   Pierre Joris, *Interglacial Narrows*
        Gabriele Tinti, *Bleedings — Incipit Tragœdia*
        Évelyne Grossman, *The Creativity of the Crisis*
        Rainer J. Hanshe, *Closing Melodies*
        Kari Hukkila, *One Thousand & One*
2024   Antonin Artaud, *Journey to Mexico*

SOME FORTHCOMING TITLES

Léon-Paul Fargue, *High Solitude*
Amina Saïd, *Walking the Earth*

AGRODOLCE SERIES

2020   Dejan Lukić, *The Oyster*
2022   Ugo Tognazzi, *The Injester*

HYPERION
On the Future of Æsthetics   2006–PRESENT

To read samples and order current & back issues of *Hyperion*,
visit contramundumpress.com/hyperion
Edited by Rainer J. Hanshe & Erika Mihálycsa (2014 ~)

 **CONTRA MUNDUM PRESS**

is published by Rainer J. Hanshe
Typography & Design: Alessandro Segalini
Publicity & Marketing: Alexandra Gold
Fundraising & Grant Writing: Madeline Hausmann
Ebook Design: Carlie R. Houser

THE FUTURE OF KULCHUR

THE PROJECT

From major museums like the MoMA to art house cinemas such as Film Forum, cultural organizations do not sustain themselves from sales alone, but from subscriptions, donations, benefactors, and grants.

Since benefactors of Peggy Guggenheim's stature are rare to come by, and receiving large grants from major funding bodies is an infrequent and unreliable source of capital, we seek to further our venture through a form of modest support that is within everyone's reach.

Although esteemed, Contra Mundum is an independent boutique press with modest profit margins. In not having university, state, or institutional backing, other forms of sustenance are required to move us into the future.

Additionally, in the past decade, the reduction of the purchasing budgets across the nation of both public and private libraries has had a severe impact upon publishers, leading to significant decreases in sales, thereby necessitating the creation of alternative means of subsistence.

Because many of our books are translations, our desire for proper remuneration is a persistent point of concern. Even when translators receive grants for book projects, the amount is often insufficient to compensate for their efforts, and royalties, which trickle in slowly over years, are not a reliable source of compensation.

WHAT WILL BE DONE

With your participation we seek to offer writers and translators greater compensation for their work, and in a more expeditious manner.

Additionally, funds will be used to pay for translation rights, basic operating expenses of the press, and to represent our writers and translators at book fairs.

If the means exist, we will also create a translation residency, providing opportunities to both junior and more established translators, thereby furthering our cultural efforts.

Through a greater collective and the cultural commons of the world, we can band together to create this constellation and together function as a patron for the writers and artists published by CMP. We hope you will join us in this partnership.

Your patronage is an expression of your confidence and belief in visionary literary work that would otherwise be exiled from the Anglophone world. With bookstores and presses around the world struggling to survive, and many even closing, joining the Future of Kulchur allows you to be a part of an active force that forms a continuous & stable foundation which safeguards the longevity of Contra Mundum Press.

Endowed by your support, we can expand our poetics of hospitality by continuing to publish works from many different languages and reflect, welcome, and embrace the riches of other cultures throughout the world. To become a member of any of our Future of Kulchur tiers is to express your support of such cultural work, and to aid us in continuing it. A unified assemblage of individuals can make a modern Mæcenas and deepen access to radical works.

The Oyster ($2/month)

- Three issues (PDFs) of your choice of our art journal, *Hyperion*.
- 15% discount on all purchases (for orders made directly through our site) during the subscription term (one year).
- Impact: $2 a month contributes to the cost to convert a title to an ebook and make it accessible to wider audiences.

Paris Spleen ($5/month)

- Receive $35 worth of books or your choice from our back catalog.
- Three issues (PDFs) of your choice of our art journal, *Hyperion*.
- 18% discount on all purchases (for orders made directly through our site) during the subscription term (one year).
- Impact: $5 a month contributes to the cost purchasing new fonts for expanding the range of our typesetting palette.

Gilgamesh ($10/month)

- Receive $70 worth books of your choice from our back catalog.
- 4 PDF issues of our magazine *Hyperion*.
- A quarterly newsletter with exclusive content such as interviews with authors or translators, excerpts from upcoming titles, publication news, and more.
- 20% discount on all merchandise (for orders made directly through our site) during the subscription term (one year).
- Select images of our books as they are being typeset.
- Impact: $10 a month contributes to the production and publication of *Hyperion*, encouraging critical engagement with art theory & æsthetics and ensuring we can pay our contributors.

The Greek Music Drama ($25/month)

- Receive $215 worth of books.
- 5 PDF issues of *Hyperion* ($25 value).
- A quarterly newsletter with exclusive content such as interviews with authors or translators, excerpts from upcoming titles, publication news, and more.
- 25% discount (for orders made directly through our site) on all merchandise during the subscription term (one year).
- Impact: $25 a month contributes to the cost of designing and formatting a book.

Citizen Above Suspicion ($50/month)

- Receive $525 worth of books.
- 6 PDF issues of *Hyperion* ($30 value).
- 1 tote.
- A quarterly newsletter with exclusive content such as interviews with authors or translators, excerpts from upcoming titles, publication news, and more.
- 30% discount on all merchandise (for orders made directly through our site) during the subscription term (one year).
- Select one forthcoming book from our catalog and receive it in advance of release to the general public.
- Impact: $50 a month contributes to editorial & proofreading fees.

Casanova ($100/month)

- Receive $1040 worth of books.
- 7 PDF issues of *Hyperion* ($30 value).
- 1 tote.
- A quarterly newsletter with exclusive content such as interviews with authors or translators, excerpts from upcoming titles, publication news, and more.
- 35% discount on all merchandise (for orders made directly through our site) during the subscription term (one year).
- A signed typeset spread from two forthcoming books.
- Select two forthcoming books from our catalog and receive them in advance of release to the general public.
- Impact: $100 a month contributes to the cost of translating a book, therefore supporting a translator in their craft & bringing a new work & perspective to Anglophone audiences.

CYBERNETOGAMIC VAMPIRE ($200/month)

- Receive $2020 worth of books.
- 10 PDF issues of *Hyperion* ($50 value).
- 1 tote.
- A quarterly newsletter with exclusive content such as interviews with authors or translators, excerpts from upcoming titles, publication news, and more.
- 40% discount on all merchandise (for orders made directly through our site) during the subscription term (one year).
- A signed typeset spread from four of our forthcoming books.
- The listing of your name in the colophon to a forthcoming book of your choice.
- Select four forthcoming books from our catalog and receive them in advance of release to the general public.
- Impact: $200 a month contributes to general operating expenses of the press, paying for translation rights, and attending book fairs to represent our writers and translators and reach more readers around the world.

To join the Future of Kulchur, visit here:

contramundumpress.com/support-us